THE
CLOUD
OF
UNKNOWING

A NEW TRANSLATION
OF A CLASSIC GUIDE
TO SPIRITUAL EXPERI-
ENCE REVEALING THE
DYNAMICS OF THE INNER
LIFE FROM A PARTICULAR
HISTORICAL AND RELI-
GIOUS POINT OF VIEW.

THE
CLOUD
OF
UNKNOWING

INTRODUCTORY COMMENTARY
AND TRANSLATION BY

IRA PROGOFF

A DELTA BOOK

A DELTA BOOK

Published by
DELL PUBLISHING CO., INC.
1 Dag Hammarskjold Plaza
New York, N.Y. 10017

Copyright © 1957, by Ira Progoff

Delta ® TM 755118, Dell Publishing Co., Inc.

ISBN: 0-440-51357-X

Reprinted by arrangement with The Julian Press, Inc.

Printed in the United States of America.

Fifth printing—March 1980

This is a book of contemplation called
The Cloud of Unknowing
in which a soul is united with God.

Ira Progoff is the author of

THE CLOUD OF UNKNOWING (a modern rendering)

THE DEATH AND REBIRTH OF PSYCHOLOGY

DEPTH PSYCHOLOGY AND MODERN MAN

JUNG'S PSYCHOLOGY AND ITS SOCIAL MEANING

THE SYMBOLIC AND THE REAL

CONTENTS

INTRODUCTORY
COMMENTARY

MORE THAN ANY OTHER, the present period of history should have a humble and open-minded attitude toward all possible sources of knowledge. Modern man has lived to see the most productive discoveries drawn from previously rejected materials. Under the hand of science, fungi and molds have been found to be sources of healing substances. Again and again in a variety of ways we are reminded of the saying of Jesus that the stone which has been cast aside will become the cornerstone. The experience of modern man has shown this to be the case on many different levels of existence, reinforcing an old rabbinic interpretation of the remark attributed to King David, "From all my teachers have I gotten understanding"; for wisdom may be drawn even—yes, especially—from the simplest events and from the least respected persons.

I begin with comments like these because I am about to ask the modern scientific individual to regard seriously, in order to learn from, a class of literature that has long been rejected. This type of literature, I must warn in advance, has even been labeled with that nasty epithet of the rationalist era, "mystic"—as though man's reason has any greater goal than to penetrate the clouded *mysteries* of human existence. That epithet, however, should not stop our turning to such a source for information and insights of an objective and productive kind; especially since this kind of material will eventually contribute significantly to the modern, rational attempt to build a science of man.

The particular text that is presented in this volume in a new translation—a translation, that is to say, from archaic English to modern English—is derived from a medieval manuscript written in fourteenth century England. It is generally classified within a special genre of medieval religious literature; and up until now, partly because of its archaic language and style, its readership has consisted mainly of individuals with highly specialized tastes and interests. Those who know of *The Cloud of Unknowing* and treasure it are to be found, however, within all shades of Christian opinion from the Quaker to the Catholic. On the one hand, we see its mark in the writings of Rufus Jones and Howard Brinton; and on the other hand, reaching into the literary realm, we see its significant influence upon T. S. Eliot in the "Four Quartets."

At the present juncture of modern thought, however, for reasons which I shall soon explain, it seems highly desirable to make *The Cloud of Unknowing* available to a more general public than the small group of admirers who have valued it in the past. We now possess, thanks to the new insights emerging from the study of depth psychology, an approach to "outdated" manuscripts such as *The Cloud of Unknowing* that makes them alive again with meaning and usefulness for man not limited by the times and circumstances in which they were written. *The Cloud of Unknowing*, for example, proceeds in terms of symbols and concepts that are, at least on the surface, far removed from the ways of thinking of the modern mind. But, underneath the seemingly vast differences between the medieval and modern images of the universe, we find an underlying sameness of searching and experience that can significantly enlarge our areas of awareness. A first step is to make texts of this kind available in more easily readable form, rephrased in the language of modern speech. This is a necessary preliminary step. With such texts at hand, it should be possible to proceed in the further experiencing and evaluation of the doctrines contained in *The Cloud of Unknowing* and in comparable manuscripts of other cultures and traditions.

PSYCHOLOGICAL SCIENCE AND THE SPIRITUAL NEED OF MODERN MAN

The past two generations have witnessed an ever-growing desire to develop a science of psychology. This desire has been symptomatic of many things, especially of the profound social and spiritual restlessness that has become one of the main characteristics of the present period in western civilization. What has been called the historical "crisis of our age" makes its presence felt in many ways, but its most immediate and most intensely felt effect is the oppressive sense of personal confusion that it visits upon individual human beings. Individuals in modern times are beset by a feeling that they do not know *who* they are or *what* they are. And they have in the background of their minds a

3

vague feeling, which is also a true intuition, that their lives are deprived both of meaning and of pleasure because they are without this knowledge.

Seeking this understanding of themselves, many have turned with great hopefulness to the young science of psychology. There is indeed a strong possibility that eventually when it has attained its maturity as the science and art dealing with the full magnitude of human personality, psychology will truly fulfill the great expectations with which modern man has turned to it. But meanwhile we should not permit the flurries of enthusiasm engendered by its early achievements to lead us into thinking that psychology is yet in a position to carry out even the main part of what the human situation in our time requires of it. A very great deal of work that is fundamentally new both in content and point of view remains to be done. In fact, one of the main reasons for presenting and commenting upon *The Cloud of Unknowing* is to indicate an important and suggestive source of the materials that psychology should study in its search for more adequate insights into the nature of the human personality.

Modern man has turned to psychology out of the fullness of a serious personal need; and it is a need that is more than personal but historical and spiritual as well. In certain areas of its development, psychology has recognized the large dimensions of the spiritual need of modern man; but the overwhelming tendency has been for it to drift in another direction.

Freud set the predominant tone of psychological work with his neurological emphasis on pathology, and with his reductive, self-analytical procedure. In the course of the first half of the twentieth century, this attitude of analytical self-consciousness has seeped into the mentality of our time to a degree that has led more than one author to refer to the modern period as a predominantly "psychological era." When we consider the situation in perspective, however, we realize that the absorption of the psychoanalytical point of view into the thought of our times represents only an early and transitory phase in the development of modern man's knowledge of himself.

Man's psychological awareness in modern times began with psychoanalysis; but it does not end with that. There are many indications that Freud, as an originator of a way of thinking, led the way into fields of study that will eventually yield fruits he did not know were planted there. This work of harvesting new understanding belongs to the second half of the twentieth century. It leads beyond the conceptions with which psychoanalysis began; and now that Freud's intimate life story has been disclosed,* we have convincing evidence that, had Freud known the full richness of the field he had discovered, he would have been as interested in its spiritual exploration as the new generation of psychologists is bound to be.

The contemporary interest in psychoanalytical types of thinking is to be understood, in the first place, as a spontaneous effort to locate and understand the Self of the individual human being in the historical flux of modern times. It is an attempt at self-knowledge; but more than that, and very significantly, it is a seeking for knowledge that will be presented within the frame of reference of

---

* See Ernest Jones, *The Life and Work of Sigmund Freud*, New York: Basic Books, 3 volumes.

science. The modern individual is pressed by his inner need to venture toward an understanding of his psychological depths. But he wishes to achieve this self-understanding upon a basis that will be—or will at least seem to be—as solid and as secure as the knowledge of his body that the medical doctor brings him by the light of biochemistry. Modern man comes with deep human problems to be answered; and he wishes to have his uncertainties resolved by an understanding of himself that will have the authority of science behind it.

Psychologists as a whole have not only acknowledged the validity of this desire, but they have also felt it very strongly in themselves. As a result, psychological studies in the twentieth century have taken special pains in attempting to satisfy the requirements of scientific method as a standard for objective truth. In rather self-conscious ways, psychologists have often gone to great extremes in this regard. In their efforts to carry out laboratory procedures to the ultimate of correctness, they occasionally give the impression that they are performing scientific method in ritual detail and with religious overzealousness. Anxious to demonstrate that they are at least as "scientific" as anyone, they lean over backward in their terminology and in the way they structure their research. And leaning over backward sometimes makes intellectual somersaults unavoidable.

Any impartial observer must recognize the fact that there are major obstacles now preventing a scientific exploration of the full dimensions of human personality with the scope and flexibility necessary for such investigations. It is a problem that is inherent in the subject matter itself.

The components of human psychology are exceedingly difficult to study in a dispassionate and verifiable way without missing subjective nuances that are of crucial importance. The great task—which stands as a major challenge before modern psychology—is to bring about a harmonious union of methodology and subject matter.

On the one hand, a full commitment to scientific method and objectivity is a prerequisite for an attempt to understand the nature of the human personality in modern times, and the spirit of science must be held to unswervingly. On the other hand, we are faced with the objective fact that man's mind and emotions, both conscious and unconscious, are such intangible, mercurial entities that they persistently elude intellectual grasp and scientific study. It is more than coincidence that, in certain psychological treatises of prescientific times, mercury was taken as a symbol of the depths of human personality.

Because of the difficulty in studying the unconscious processes of the mind objectively, some have claimed that the hope of developing a scientific psychology is ultimately an unfulfillable aspiration. Psychology can be scientific, it has been said, only at the cost of its subject matter. It can be scientific only if it eliminates from its sphere of study those subjects of investigation that elude laboratory experiments and statistical correlation. But if it does that, it will be omitting the very problems that psychology is called upon to solve. If it would become scientific at that cost, psychology would be reneging on its obligation to modern man. It would be giving up the goal just at the point where it was looked to most expectantly for significant help. It would fail to bring to modern man the insight into the intangible depths of personality that is essential for renewed human development in our time.

It would seem that psychology can fulfill its role in modern civilization only if it manages to meet both sides of this apparent dilemma in a constructive and integrative way. Psychology must retain its commitment to science, conceiving it as a dedication to objective study. At the same time it must address itself without hedging and without retreat to the full range of issues that arise in the study of the magnitude of the human personality, no matter how difficult and delicate those issues may prove to be.

There are a number of steps that can be taken in meeting this twofold requirement of psychological study. Here, however, I would like to make one main suggestion. It is that while psychology maintains its adherence to high standards of objective scientific study, it should at the same time significantly expand its range of subjects.

The spirit of science requires that every disciplined striving for knowledge must include all the data relevant to its field of investigation. It is therefore essential that psychologists study the nervous system, the patterns of habit formation, learning procedures, and all the other aspects of human behavior. But it is also essential to remember that psychology is the science devoted primarily to the study of the *psyche*, that is, to the processes that operate *within* the human personality.

These processes may be described in terms that fit the sciences that deal with more tangible factors and in which "cause" and "effect" are more readily observed; sciences such as biology, physics, and chemistry. A very large part of modern psychological theory represents an attempt to apply the explanatory principles of these sciences in the study of psychological phenomena. We see this, for example, in the conception of the "mechanisms" underlying conscious thought and unconscious emotionality. Such descriptions, however, apply only to a particular level of human functioning. They do not describe the more creative and also self-directive processes by which individuals, in nonmechanistic ways, seek to achieve a fuller development and realization of the capacities of the psyche.

The self-directed development of the faculties of the inner life has been almost entirely neglected in the modern study of psychology. The fundamental reason for this neglect, it would seem, is that the disciplines of personal psychological development have mainly been carried through within the frames of reference of various religious or philosophical ideologies. Those who seek to find the objective "mechanisms" of the psyche and who follow, consciously or not, a personal ideology of materialism in one variation or another, feel something alien in such procedures. They react against them emotionally, castigate them as "spiritual," and dismiss them as nonscientific. The profound psychological significance of the many and varied disciplines of personality development is thus altogether missed. The evidence is dismissed peremptorily, simply by disdaining to discuss the subject. Thus, in the name of science, a most unscientific act is committed; and the science of psychology is deprived of a source of information and insight that can contribute greatly to the task of understanding the dynamic processes at work in the inner life of man.

We must consider this last point very seriously. Until

now, the advance of psychology as a science has been seriously impeded by the fact that it has not been able to deal scientifically with the subtle, seemingly subjective experiences of the human person. The experiences of the spirit, the creative moments of religion and art, are intangible and difficult to analyze. They are strange and frightening to the temperament, the "psychological type," and intellectual habit of mind of the dedicated laboratory experimenter and statistic-gatherer.

Nonetheless, temperamental aversions placed to one side, we should not overlook the striking fact that experimental work has been going on for many, many centuries in the understanding and channeling of the dynamic processes of man's inner life. These experiments have not been "controlled" in the modern sense; nor have they provided quantitative data. But, by a persistent, cumulative gathering and testing of personal experience, through individual trial and error over the years, by reflecting, reconsidering, and reattempting the work, a process of experimentation in the disciplined development of the personality has been carried on and a body of knowledge has been accumulated.

This knowledge is scattered in many traditions and is both concealed and conveyed in the symbolism of many religious and cultish doctrines. Because of the diversity of its symbolic forms, it is a knowledge that is not easily available to modern man; but it could be made available to him, intelligibly and usefully, if the science of psychology in whose province it belongs would take the trouble to study it, interpret it, and apply its findings scientifically.

If modern psychologists would turn their attention to

studying some of the early records of disciplined psychological undertakings, they would soon realize that those prescientific men were working in a spirit of science not unlike their own, imbued with a high regard for the empirical testing of objective psychological truth. The modern psychologist would then see that those early experimenters in psychological development were engaged in the immediate and personal kind of experimentation that is a necessity peculiar to the subject matter of psychology, i.e., the psyche or inner life of man. We could then find that those men, often labeled "mystics," were actually precursors and models for the development of a modern scientific psychology dedicated to the inner growth of personality. And when the modern work of interpretation would be far enough advanced, we would find that we had drawn from the hard-won "spiritual" knowledge of the centuries the basis for new psychological conceptions that would provide a more ample and more realistic awareness of the capacities of human personality.

THE MODERN RENDERING
OF THE CLOUD OF UNKNOWING

It was with this purpose in mind that I undertook the study of *The Cloud of Unknowing*. It had been called to my attention as a particularly sensitive, realistic, and objective description of the experimental work of the inner life, as dealt with from a particular type of historical and religious point of view. The text at first reading impressed me as being most significant for modern psychological understanding. As I went more deeply into the work, I found that many words that I had thought I understood in the fourteenth-century text had acquired different meanings since the day when the book was written. Words that are still in existence and are even in common use today were used with radically different connotations in the original text. Since these meanings had long been obsolete I did not know of them; and I assume that the same is the case for most other modern readers. Because these words are in use today I attributed their modern meaning to them; and I was often in error where I least suspected it.

Considering these things, I came to the conclusion that if my study was to lead to an intelligible and valid interpretation of the text, a first and essential step would be to render it into modern language, if only for my own use. It appeared also that it would be quite desirable to work out a modern rendering of the text for the benefit of the general reader who might turn to *The Cloud of Unknowing* with something other than a psychological interest.

The original text of *The Cloud of Unknowing* was written in the language of daily life in fourteenth-century England. The purpose of the book was to provide practical advice for all individuals interested in achieving a direct knowledge of God that they might verify by their own experience. Accordingly, the author addressed himself neither to the academic men nor to the clergy, but he spoke rather to the generality of mankind, to all persons whatever their station or condition in life, whether male or female, learned or illiterate, whoever might read the book or have it read to them.

The author's one requirement of his readers was that they feel a strong and sincere desire for a direct meeting with God in the spirit. This contact with God was not understood as something transcendent or removed from daily life. It was sought, rather, as a content of immediate experience, and it was thus described and referred to in the language of everyday affairs with colloquial expressions and pungent phrases, indicating that though the author was a monk he was in close touch with the secular life of his times. He was interested in reaching people on all levels of society. He therefore used the terms of ordinary speech so that he might strike the largest common denominator by speaking of man's relation to God in words that everyone would be able to understand.

In order to be true to the original text, it has been essential that this modern version be rendered wherever possible into the colloquial language of everyday speech. Otherwise one could get an entirely erroneous impression of *The Cloud of Unknowing*. It was addressed to everyone, to everyone, that is, who felt a desire for personally proved religious conviction. Its language, therefore, was full of the tang and saltiness of everyday life.

It is certainly true that there are today a great number of persons who enjoy reading old texts in their original, archaic styles. Perhaps the outstanding example of this is the case of those who prefer to read the Bible in the original King James version rather than the various revised and modernized renderings. Such individuals are usually well aware that the early King James version contains many misleading and erroneous translations, but they are primarily interested in something else. They want to make an affirmative religious use of the fact that the outmoded language and style of that version of the Bible carries for them many rich associations with their childhood. They want to restore the memories attached to their early reading of the Bible and to experience again the beauty of its literary rhythms. And this certainly has great merit and validity in its own right. It is obviously not, however, an approach to the Bible in terms of the intrinsic content of the text.

The case of *The Cloud of Unknowing* is altogether different from this, for *The Cloud of Unknowing* is by no means a center of family worship as the Bible is for many persons. It is a profound text with many veiled meanings that have to be understood as deeply and as clearly as possible if the point of the book is to be grasped and if the personal experience it seeks is actually to be achieved.

In fact, the essential aim of the spiritual work that *The Cloud of Unknowing* describes requires that the individual be led beyond the associations and emotionality of childhood to the most mature religious experience possible. While it demands great fervor of spiritual feeling, *The Cloud of Unknowing* moves on a level that is beyond emotional dependence on childhood memories and family traditions. It appeals to our mature understanding—not merely to our intellectual, but to our spiritual understanding—and for this a keen discernment in language is necessary as a tool of knowledge.

In working out this modern rendition, I have made use of three main versions of the original text published in recent times. They are those of Evelyn Underhill, published by John M. Watkins in London; by Abbot Justin McCann, O.S.B., published by The Newman Press, Westminster, Maryland; and by Phyllis Hodgson, the closest to the original manuscript, published under the auspices of The Early English Text Society of London. To each of these editors and to their publishers, I tender my great and sincere appreciation.*

These three versions provided me with a kind of consensus against which to check my modern rendition. In general I have held to the original text of *The Cloud of Unknowing* as closely as possible while replacing old words with new ones to convey the author's meaning. I have also restructured the sentences wherever necessary in order to make certain that the free flow of the thought would not be hindered by archaic syntax. At various points in the text, however, the reader will find that obsolete words have been deliberately retained. These are words that have gone out of currency but which have a special pungency and impact in the form in which the author employs them. Wherever possible, I have left the original phrases in such cases, and my criterion has been to see whether the meaning of the word becomes clear from the immediate context in which it appears. In such cases I have substituted another word only when the phrase was used in a different sense or in a different context. Throughout, the aim has been to capture and convey the spirit of the original document so that the modern reader can feel sympathetically, and perhaps experience for himself, what the author was trying to say and trying to do.

One innovation in this version that should be noted

* *The Cloud of Unknowing*, Edited and with an Introduction by Evelyn Underhill, London: John M. Watkins, 1912; *The Cloud of Unknowing*, edited by Abbot Justin McCann, O.S.B., Westminster, Md.: The Newman Press, 1924; *The Cloud of Unknowing*, edited by Phyllis Hodgson, published for The Early English Text Society by Oxford University Press, London, 1944.

particularly is the numbering of the paragraphs. The text consists of seventy-five chapters, and I have numbered the paragraphs within each chapter, sometimes breaking the long paragraphs into two or three shorter ones. It has seemed to me that to number the paragraphs will provide a convenient and practical way to refer to particular sections of the text for study and comment. For example, without reference to page number, the fourth paragraph in the thirty-eighth chapter may simply be referred to for standard reference as XXXVIII:4.

THE AUTHOR AND THE GOAL OF HIS WORK

The information available to us concerning the author and background of *The Cloud of Unknowing* is lacking in detail. The best scholarship on the subject indicates that it was the work of a monk who lived in England, probably in the east central part, during the middle of the fourteenth century. He wrote anonymously, and in all likelihood he did so not out of modesty but out of prudence.

In the fourteenth century, the ecclesiastical authorities were sedulously in search of heresy; for a number of small, unorthodox, highly individualized spiritual groups were active throughout western Europe during that period. Perhaps the most significant step was taken in the year 1329 when the conceptions set forth by Meister Eckhart were officially condemned by the Pope. Eckhart's writings and sermons represented the most advanced expression of the antiformalistic point of view in that time. His approach to religion emphasized the importance of independent inquiry and individual experience; and this was a point of view to which the author of *The Cloud of Unknowing* was also strongly committed.

The underlying attitudes of Meister Eckhart and the author of *The Cloud of Unknowing* have a great deal in common; and it is perhaps just because of this closeness—and the consequent nearness of the Inquisitor as well—that the author of *The Cloud of Unknowing* constantly avows his horror of all forms of heresy. We do not know whether he was ever formally charged with heresy himself; but, at the very best, he must have lived a precarious existence if his authorship was known during his lifetime. It was only in later generations that the Roman Catholic Church recognized the legitimacy of this direct, personal approach to religious experience and gave it official sanction and encouragement.

The thirteenth century with its encompassing synthesis of reason and faith as composed by Saint Thomas Aquinas had brought everything into order. Religious knowledge had reached its highest point according to the official pronouncement of the time; but the interesting fact is that the period directly after the generation of Saint Thomas, in direct contrast to the systematized, reasonable orderliness of Thomas's integration, was a time of spiritual turbulence in which the most varied mystical movements mushroomed all through Europe from England to Italy.

The system that the Scholastics had proclaimed does not seem to have sufficed for many of the Roman Catholic brethren of the time. They felt a pressing need to come close to God directly and spontaneously in terms of the intense immediacy of their individual religious promptings.

This aspect of the fourteenth century has been referred to aptly by Rufus Jones as "the flowering of mysticism," and while it was strongest in the German-speaking areas of Europe, it was actively developed in England as well. The author of *The Cloud of Unknowing* seems to have been one of the most energetic, and certainly one of the most competent figures in this period of spiritual ferment and controversy in medieval Christianity. He wrote several tracts, all of which are anonymous, but which we nevertheless are able to identify with confidence because of their distinctive style and point of view. *The Cloud of Unknowing* stands out, however, as his most important work. It is the one that expresses most articulately the principles of his teaching and in which the meaning of his personal "experiment with truth" is most impressively conveyed.

It seems certain that our unknown author was a monk of some denomination; but there is no agreement as to the specific order to which he belonged. The fact that he spent the last years of his life in monastic seclusion seems to be indicated by the tone of his writings; but it is considered probable that he was a secular priest, and that perhaps in his younger years he was not a priest at all.

One of the most intriguing aspects of *The Cloud of Unknowing* and the other writings of its author is their blunt and earthy tone. They were obviously not the work of a man who had confined himself to a monastic ivory tower. Quite the contrary, they seem to have been written by a person who was particularly familiar with the frailties of human nature, and who was capable of accepting people as they were.

The author of *The Cloud of Unknowing* impresses the modern reader again and again with his sharp, profound, amazingly perceptive insights into man's psychological limitations. He was by no means a tender-minded individual, as the authors of mystical treatises frequently tend to be. Just the opposite, indeed. *The Cloud of Unknowing* was written by someone who was exceedingly tough-minded in the sense in which William James used the phrase. He was most unsentimental, matter of fact, and down to earth; and he regarded this habit of mind as a prerequisite for the work in which he was engaged. He proceeded upon the belief that when an individual undertakes to bring his life into relation to God, he is embarking upon a serious and demanding task, a task that leaves no leeway for self-deception or illusion. It requires the most rigorous dedication and self-knowledge. *The Cloud of Unknowing* is therefore a book of strong and earnest thinking. It makes a realistic appraisal of the problems and weaknesses of individual human beings, for it regards man's imperfections as the raw material to be worked with in carrying out the discipline of spiritual development.

The author states that the specific purpose for which he was writing *The Cloud of Unknowing* was to provide guidance for a young man twenty-four years of age who was seriously considering taking a step that would commit him to a life of religious dedication as a *Contemplative*. Ostensibly the book is written for this young man personally to help him reach a decision by indicating the kinds of persons who are capable of leading such a life, and what it involves for them in practice.

One feels, however, that this situation was used largely

as a literary device to provide a frame of reference for the theme. The necessity of giving this piece of advice presented a convenient occasion for describing in detail a point of view with which its author was deeply involved. Also, in the course of rendering his "advice," the author has described various experiences of his own, indicating that he was doing something more than set forth the psychological outlines of a religious discipline. He was satisfying a need of his own for a personal confession concerning the unconventional, highly individualized, and certainly lonely work in which he had been engaged. It is this personal confession, inadvertently revealed, that gives *The Cloud of Unknowing* its impressive tone of sincerity and spiritual intensity; and it also provides a main reason for our believing in the personal authenticity of the work.

As the life of contemplation is referred to in the text, it seems to imply complete withdrawal from the world. The author indicates, however, that there is no rigid requirement. A wide flexibility is possible in the work, for there are several levels at which the life of the contemplative can be experienced. He makes the more basic point as well that it is not the physical withdrawal from the secular world into the cloister that is the essential thing. What is more important is the withdrawal of psychological attachments from individual entities, objects, and relationships. The implication then is present in the text that the life of contemplation and union with God may involve the fully isolated monastic life, or it may not. Either path may lead to the ultimate goal, and in varying degrees. Grace and the spontaneous love of God are more important than any of the physical conditions of life. The author develops this point in the most subtle ways, and occasionally with remarkable brilliance, even at several points reminding us of the elastic strength and wisdom found in the Japanese masters of Zen and the Hasidic Zaddiks who appeared in European Judaism a few centuries after *The Cloud of Unknowing* was written.

The term *contemplative* carries overtones of passivity and of withdrawal from the vortex of life; but it has a much more active meaning in *The Cloud of Unknowing*. To speak of undertaking to live as a *Contemplative*—as was the young man to whom the author was addressing his instructions—referred, in the frame of reference of the fourteenth century, to a special way of life. The *Contemplative* was a person who undertook, either within a monastery or in secular living, to control his thoughts and feelings by means of special disciplines in order to become capable of a closer relationship with God. Far from being passive, then, the contemplative life is decidedly active, for it involves a most ambitious spiritual enterprise.

There are, however, several obstacles that hinder the modern reader who tries to conceive within the terms of his present situation what the *contemplative life* would mean in practice. For one thing, the descriptions of this way are presented in *The Cloud of Unknowing* within the frame of reference of the medieval view of the world; and many of the conceptions that it takes for granted are strange indeed to the modern mind. It was, after all, before the day of Copernicus and Gallileo, before the appearance of the modern forms of economy and political life, when western culture was still in a rudimentary stage. It was a time also when Europe was steeped in religiosity, when Satan, the Saints, and the Sacraments were ever-present realities of daily life for practically everyone.

In those days, whatever else one would do, the religious forms and observances had to be included, and a certain degree of deference had to be accorded them. The secularization of western society, which was to bring a radically different style of thinking to modern man, had not yet begun to show itself. It is necessary, therefore, if we wish to understand the creative activity expressed in the *contemplative life* as *The Cloud of Unknowing* describes it, to divest ourselves temporarily of our habitual mode of thinking and see the world from a premodern point of view.

This transformation of mentality from the modern to the medieval is not as difficult as might be expected, at least not where *The Cloud of Unknowing* is concerned. The reason is, I think, that it works toward its spiritual experience on psychologically neutral ground, where the modern and medieval individual can meet and understand each other not in terms of their historical differences, but in terms of the sameness of their essential quest. All that is necessary to keep this common ground in view is a recognition that the author's central aim was to achieve a unity with God that would transcend time, place, and social circumstances.

This meeting ground is established in a significant way. The author of *The Cloud of Unknowing* describes the discipline of the contemplative life within the framework of the Christian orthodoxy of the fourteenth century; but it soon becomes apparent that he does not consider the formal observance of ritual to be dominant. He cautions

his young student not to relax his obedience to the teachings of the Church, but that seems to be mainly a pre-
cautionary measure. He does not want the neophyte to
lose his connection with the traditional practices and insti-
tutions before he is ready to sustain himself by individual
work.

In this we can see a clear indication of the role that the
teachings of *The Cloud of Unknowing* are to play in the
individual's development. The principles and practices
described are to be followed in the advanced stages of
religious study. They are not a substitute for regular
religious observances, but they are the next step forward
for those who seek a higher degree of development. Thus,
with respect to the formal observance of prayer, he writes,
"Those who truly practice this work do not worship by
prayer very much. They pray according to the form and
the law that has been ordained by the holy fathers before
us; but their special prayers always rise spontaneously
to God without having been planned in advance, and without any particular techniques either preceding them or
accompanying them" (XXXVII:1).

The author, like most of his religious contemporaries,
lived within the frame of reference provided by the Bible.
The incidents of its stories were familiar facts to him, and
the figures in its pages were persons with whom he had
an everyday contact. As he develops the point of his
argument, therefore, he refers to these persons and events
as examples, and especially as prototypes, of the disciplines
and experiences he is discussing. He elaborates often on
the sayings of Jesus and on the life of the Virgin Mary;
and he interprets the acts of Saint Stephen, Saint Martin,

Martha and Mary, Moses, Bezaleel, and Aaron, and various doctrines of the church concerning the nature of God.

These are a necessary part of his work of instruction. But soon we realize that the references to the Bible, to Jesus, and to the nature of God have only a transitory significance. The aim of the work is to lead beyond all theological conceptions and doctrines, and beyond all attachments to religious objects and observances.

"Indeed," the author writes, "if it will be considered courteous and proper to say so, it is of little value or of no value at all in this work to think about the kindness or the great worth of God, nor of our Lady, nor of the saints or angels in heaven, nor even of the joys in heaven. It is of no value, that is to say, to hold them intently before your mind as you would do in order to strengthen and increase your purpose. I believe that it would not be helpful at all in accomplishing this work. For, even though it is good to think about the kindness of God, and to love Him and to praise Him for it, nevertheless it is far better to think about His naked being and to praise Him and to love Him for Himself" (V:3).

The ultimate goal of the work of *The Cloud of Unknowing* is union with God, not as God is thought of or as God is imagined to be, but as God *is* in His nature. And though this statement may seem to suggest a dogmatic and absolutist attitude, it is actually reasonable and flexible in its meaning. It refers to an experience in which man seems to be transcending himself, but is in fact discovering himself *as he is*. He is coming into contact with his own "naked being," and, by means of this, it becomes possible for him to come into contact with God *as He is*. This experience, which takes the form of various degrees and levels of "union" with God, is psychologically exceedingly difficult to achieve; but it is nonetheless held to be attainable by man in principle with practice as *The Cloud of Unknowing* describes.

The author begins with the observation that, before a person can reach the ground of "naked being" that is at the core of his own nature and of God's, there are many obstacles within his mind that he must overcome. Idle and misleading thoughts, chains of habit, and the stream of unconscious association must be systematically pressed down; the wanderings of the curiosity must be held in check; and the strong promptings of the imagination must be resisted. All these and more the author discusses in practical terms, suggesting a number of procedures that had been found effective in the past. He never recommends that a given technique be taken over as a whole and applied in a fixed form, but rather that it be tested by the individual and adapted to meet the needs of his special case.

The aim of these practices, which must be described as essentially psychological, is to break through the bonds that attach the individual to the world of his senses and separate him from his eternal nature. These bonds are of many kinds; but whatever their content, essentially they are thoughts, and their effect on the person is through the mind. Most especially, according to the author of *The Cloud of Unknowing*, it is *Memory* that separates man from his true self; for *Memory* has in the text an encompassing meaning as the dynamic and all-inclusive force in man's mental life that binds the mind to objects of past experience. It is, therefore, the attachments of memory that must be overcome before the individual can reach his "naked being" (LXIII:1,4; LXVII).

The attachments of memory may be of various kinds. They may be personal and principally derived from the individual's experience, both his pleasures and his pains. And they may be the products of a nonpersonal or group memory that fasten the individual's mind to symbols and doctrines preserved and extolled by religious tradition. Such images and beliefs, the author of *The Cloud of Unknowing* tells us, should not be rejected in themselves. They may be retained as the contents of conventional religion. But the individual who wishes to reach God as He is in Himself must overcome his attachment to all such beliefs, even the most hallowed. The author specifically extends this to the Sacraments and to meditations upon the life of Christ. Sacred objects are not to become stopping places, lest we remain with them and forget that our one goal is God as He is in Himself.

This teaching of *The Cloud of Unknowing* is reminiscent of one that is expressed in a rather strong form in Zen Buddhism. There, it is said, "When you have spoken the name Buddha, wash your mouth out!"

This was by no means intended as a sacrilegious statement, for the Buddha in Buddhism is as holy and revered a figure as Christ in Christianity and the Messiah in Judaism. Its significance is rather to emphasize that attachment to the symbolic forms and sacred figures of man's religions can easily become an impediment in the ultimate quest of the spirit. This quest involves each individual alone in the privacy and tension of his love and need of God. It reaches in each person from the deep core of his being to the "naked being only of God Himself"; and it does so in varying degrees, depending upon how fully one has persevered and how much one has achieved in the work.

DYNAMICS OF THE SEARCH FOR GOD

One main characteristic of the goal of this work is that it cannot be attained in the ordinary condition of human consciousness. The spiritual disciplines of many religious traditions bear testimony to this fact, in Yoga, in Zen, Hasidism, Sufism, and especially in *The Cloud of Unknowing*. In fact, the special purpose of the author was to give his disciple an understanding of the particular quality of consciousness that is required, so that he might know how to adapt to his own use the various techniques of achieving it.

The normal tendency of consciousness is to move outward toward the environment in terms of sensory contacts, social feelings, ideological beliefs, emotional attachments, and so on. This outward movement necessarily involves a spreading of attention with a consequent dissipation of the energy available to the mind (psychic energy). The first requirement of the work described in *The Cloud of Unknowing* is then to call a halt to this squandering of energy by outward diffusion; and it undertakes to accomplish this by means of disciplined attention to the activities of the mind.

Its first step is to curtail, with the aim eventually of eliminating, all the various distractions that play upon the mind. This means the control of thoughts arising from contact with other persons and objects; and the control of thoughts arising from within, fantasies and imaginings, desires and beliefs. It calls for a drawing back of all attachments or, in psychological language, of all projections whether they are valid or false, so that they will no longer be able to serve as avenues for the expenditure of energy in the world. It involves in principle a recall of all energy that is invested by the individual in objects and in thoughts of every kind.

We are reminded in this connection of Sigmund Freud's observation regarding some equivalent psychological processes. "Certain practises of mystics," he wrote, "may succeed in upsetting the normal relations between the different regions of the mind, so that, for example, the perceptual system becomes able to grasp relations in the deeper layers of the ego and the id which would otherwise be inaccessible to it." And Freud added, "We must admit that the therapeutic efforts of psycho-analysis have chosen much the same method of approach."* The difference between Sigmund Freud and the author of *The Cloud of Unknowing* is that, while Freud recognized intellectually the validity and importance of the mental processes involved, the author of *The Cloud* investigated them still further in a practical way, experimenting with them within his own personality to see empirically what would happen.

From a psychological point of view, the control of thoughts and other psychic contents together with the withdrawal of the mental energy invested in the world would inevitably result in an attrition of what Freud called the "perceptual system"; and this would mean an

---

* Sigmund Freud, *New Introductory Lectures on Psychoanalysis,* New York: W. W. Norton & Co., Inc., 1933, p. 111-112.

attrition of consciousness as a whole. This would then bring about—in the phrase of Pierre Janet, a great precursor of Freud and of modern depth psychology in general—an *"abaissement du niveau mental,"* a lowering of the mental level, with a corresponding intensification of psychic activity at the subliminal depths of the personality. C. G. Jung has referred to this in terms of his conception of the "Collective Unconscious," indicating that the "lowering of the mental level" on one side of the personality results in a concentration of energy at the deep unconscious levels that lie beneath the threshold of consciousness. A temporary condition of mental unbalance is thus created in which the individual experiences a great intensity of psychic affect. He becomes subject, then, to a generalized mental instability that results from the disordering and disturbance of psychic factors at deep mental levels. Paradoxically, this troubled activity that is beyond conscious control leads to experiences of heightened intensity, enlarged areas of awareness, and a degree both of perceptivity and of feeling far greater than the ordinary condition of consciousness would make possible. Jung's descriptions of these processes in terms of the various "levels" of the "unconscious" provide very close approximations to what takes place psychologically in the spiritual discipline set forth in *The Cloud of Unknowing.*

In the processes that *The Cloud of Unknowing* describes, the first step is a deliberate attrition of consciousness; and this is balanced by greatly increased activity at the subliminal levels of the personality. This new psychic activity, however, is not related to the outer conditions of life, and the individual engaged in this work may, at this point, seem to be out of touch with the realities of society and of his fellow men. He then discovers that his attitude of introversion all too easily leads him into conflict with other individuals who are suspicious of what he may be doing when they see him sitting silent and withdrawn. Particularly if these people are of an "extraverted" type, and if they have not themselves felt a call to undertake some inner discipline, they will feel either that he is remiss in his obligations to others, perhaps just plain lazy; or worse, since he has an attitude of personal abstraction as though he has been distracted from life with his attention drawn far away from the objects immediately around him, they will feel that he is mentally pathologic. It would seem, to judge from the text, that the author of *The Cloud of Unknowing* had considerable unpleasant experience of this kind with his neighbors, for he discusses with great feeling the problems of individuals who undertake to carry out the contemplative discipline in the midst of people who are not sympathetic to, and do not understand the nature of, the contemplative life. The passages dealing with Mary and Martha are particularly instructive on this subject. They present a frank, unguarded expression of the author's feelings in a way that is personally touching, and psychologically revealing of the problems of his life (XVII-XXI).

The author warns his disciple that he may experience a temporary but highly inconvenient side-effect while carrying on his work. He will, almost inevitably, display a certain distractedness and lack of contact with his immediate environment. This will be a difficult and distressing moment for him; but it is essentially a transitory condition, if the disciple does not give up but perseveres in his work.

Eventually, contact with his surroundings will be restored; and the author even assures his disciple that if he carries the work far towards fulfillment, he will find "that it regulates his conduct so agreeably, both in body and in soul, that it will make him most attractive to every man or woman who sees him." It will even make him "well able to render judgment, if the need should arise, for people of all natures and dispositions." And, in contrast to his earlier distractedness, it will make him "well able to bring himself into harmony with all those who come into contact with him" (LIV:1,2). This promise of greater human capacities for persons who carry out the work to its goal is based upon the principle that whoever achieves union with God will thereby manifest this unity in his personal bearing among mankind.

The passing phase of the work, in which the disciple is distracted from life with his conscious orientation upset, is an understandable phenomenon when considered from a psychological point of view. It reflects the fact that, with the individual's psychic energy withdrawn into the subliminal depths of the personality, the attention to life in its outer, more conventional aspects is necessarily impaired.

From a psychological point of view, this pattern of experience is highly similar to that undergone by the disciple in Zen Buddhism who seeks to attain enlightenment (*Satori*) by means of the *Koan* method. The *Koan* is an imponderable conundrum, a mind-breaking problem given to the Zen disciple by his master with the purpose of shocking him into *Satori* through a realization of the illogic and paradox inherent in life, and the unity of Being underlying all things. An example of a *Koan* would be: "What are your original features which you have even prior to your birth?" or "Listen to the sound of one hand."*

When he receives his *Koan*, the disciple directs himself toward finding a solution. He has been instructed to proceed by means of his "abdomen" rather than his "head." That is to say, the master advises him to seek to solve his problem not by conscious or intellectual reasoning, but out of the subliminal levels of his mind without the use of consciousness. This advice, we notice, is the same as that given by the author of *The Cloud of Unknowing*.

The Zen disciple then concentrates ever more intently upon solving his *Koan*. He draws his energy down into his abdomen (his unconscious), and by so doing he steadily decreases the amount of energy available for his conscious activities. A psychological condition of *abaissement* then comes into effect; it is a lowering of the mental level, and this causes the disciple's behavior to become dangerously distracted and insecure. Viewed from the outside, he seems to be out of touch with his surroundings and lost in a schizophrenic state. Viewed from the inside, he is altogether encased in his task of finding a solution for an unanswerable problem. His entire being is concentrated upon this single point, and he drives forward upon it with such intensity that he is not aware of himself at all and

---

* See D. T. Suzuki, *Zen Buddhism*, New York: Anchor Books, 1956, Chap. VI; *see also* D. T. Suzuki, *An Introduction to Zen Buddhism*, New York: Philosophical Library, 1949, Chap. VIII.

does not know what he is doing. It is as though he is covered over in a mist. His eyes are closed and he goes forward blindly. Now he is walking across the proverbial razor's edge without being able to see, without even thinking to look where he is stepping. On either side lies psychosis; somewhere, wherever the interminable razor's edge ends; there lies *Satori.*

Then, suddenly, there comes a shell-breaking insight, a spontaneous outcry. Having been completely lost to himself and unaware of what he was doing, the Zen disciple has found the greater Self he originally came to seek. He can now return to his former station in life, the same person, but altogether different.

From this brief description, we can follow the psychological parallel between the Zen disciple and person who seeks enlightenment by means of *The Cloud of Unknowing.* Both begin their work by withdrawing their attention from their surroundings and by concentrating their energies within themselves. A psychological consequence of this is that the social contacts that ordinarily stimulate conscious development now dwindle.

The individual's conscious activities steadily diminish and grow weaker at this point. His awareness of himself grows dim. He continues in his work; that is, he continues in his effort to solve the problem he has set himself regarding the paradox of existence; to discover how man, separated by nature from God, can yet achieve unity with God. But he goes about this difficult work as though he were without any conscious guidance. He is, in fact, hardly conscious at all that he is doing anything. He goes on with his labors; indeed, he is altogether engaged in them and he works with great intensity, but he also is as though covered by a mist, a cloud, a darkness that hides everything he does and hides everything that takes place within him. And "when I speak of darkness," the author of *The Cloud of Unknowing* says, it is not "the kind of darkness that is in your house at night when the candle is out." It is a darkness of a quite different kind. "I am referring," he says, "to a lack of knowing. It is a lack of knowing that includes everything you do not know or else that you have forgotten, whatever is altogether dark for you because you do not see it with your spiritual eye. And for this reason it is not called a cloud of the air, but rather a cloud of unknowing that is between you and your God" (IV:18).

This last phrase, "a cloud of unknowing that is *between* you and your God," is of particular interest. The word "between" has a twofold meaning here. On the one hand it signifies separation; on the other hand, connection. What is separating man from God is not any physical thing but the state of his consciousness. More specifically, it is man's consciousness of his separateness, of his existence as an individual apart from God that keeps him separated from God. To overcome this awareness of separateness, he must place himself in a psychological situation that weakens, and ultimately dispenses with, the conscious guidance of his personal being. He must permit himself to drop into a condition of unconsciousness, a condition of total unknowing. This encompassing state of unconsciousness is the cloud of unknowing that covers him in darkness, dulls his awareness of his separate existence, and

34

provides the medium in which his union with God may take place.

Once one is altogether covered by the darkness of the cloud of unknowing, it may happen that a light unexpectedly appears. If it does come, the author tells us, it will come "merely as a sudden stirring with no forewarning, instantly springing toward God as a spark from a coal. And," he adds, "it is wonderful to count the number of stirrings that may appear within one hour in a soul that is disposed to the work" (IV:14).

It will be "a blind stirring of love" (IV:16). "Blind," because its origin will have been in darkness, its movement will have been unconscious, and no guidance will direct it toward its goal. Yet it goes toward God, and it does so because ultimately it "is the work only of God" (XXVI:3). Despite its "blindness," it moves with *love;* and this is most essential, for "God may be reached and held close by means of love, but by means of thought never" (VI:3). Thus, this "blind stirring of love" that springs "toward God as a spark from a coal" marks the beginning of the experience of enlightenment that emerges from the cloud of unknowing.

Out of the intensity of the disciple's striving within the cloud of unknowing, a spontaneous prayer may be called forth. It will not be an eloquent prayer, but a prayer of one word, perhaps only of one syllable, such as, "God" or "Sin." It is an involuntary outcry of a person in desperation. And since this one syllable "is prayed with a full spirit, in the height and in the depth, in the length and in the breadth of the spirit of him who prays it," it reaches God and receives a reply. When it is born out of the sincere intensity of spiritual need, "short prayer pierces heaven" (XXXVII, XXXVIII).

The answer to the outcry of the disciple struggling in the darkness of the cloud of unknowing comes as an illumination. God sends him "a beam of spiritual light" which pierces the cloud of unknowing in order to reach him. And then God reveals "some of His secret ways of which man neither can nor may speak" (XXVI:5). After striving in blind unconsciousness, the disciple at last becomes able to see; and what he sees gives him knowledge, gained in his unknowing state, of a kind that no degree of ordinary consciousness could have brought him before. This is the culminating experience of his search. "The higher part of the contemplative life," the author tells us, "takes place altogether in this darkness and in the cloud of unknowing with a loving striving blindly beholding the naked being only of God Himself" (VIII:9).

What transpires in this ultimate moment may not, however, be spoken of truly as a *knowledge* of God. Neither can it accurately be called a *feeling* of God, nor even an *experience* of God. It is rather a state of unity of being that is suddenly established by which God and the individual human person are together as one. And this transformation takes place in the briefest instant. "It is the shortest work that man can imagine. It is neither longer nor shorter than an atom" (IV:2).

In this instant, out of the cloud of unknowing, a new unity comes into being. And when it is truly established, it is not merely a composite of two separate entities such as God and the individual human being; but it is a unity in which the separateness of man is obliterated in God so that oneness is established as an actual fact of existence.

But this is most difficult, and it seldom is fully achieved. If, for example, the individual *feels* or *experiences* himself as being in unity with God, that very feeling and awareness of an experience indicates that real unity has not yet been achieved. At such times, the author of *The Cloud* tells us, "If you look truly you will find," that something is still "between you and your God" (IX:1). There is still work remaining to be done.

The mere fact that the individual *feels* his presumed unity with God as a personal experience indicates that he is still separated from God. The individual who *experiences* God thereby emphasizes the duality of his own individual existence, his personal thatness, and the existence of God as separate from him. In that case it cannot be said that he knows God truly and intimately in oneness.

What the author of *The Cloud of Unknowing* seeks is thus not an experience or feeling of unity with God; but rather the establishment of a fact of existence, a condition of life, in which the individual is God—and vise versa—in actuality, even if only for the briefest atom of a moment.

At such a time, having overcome his attachments to the objects of life, the memory of past experiences and present desires, the memory and attachment to sacred figures and traditional observances, having overcome all these and whatever other thoughts of any kind may press upon the cloud of unknowing, a man comes very close to the naked being of human nature. And there, at that deepest ground

37

of his being, he is no longer an individual as such, but he participates in the naked being that is God's ultimate nature. Then oneness becomes indeed a fact of his existence; and he can say with Meister Eckhart, "the eye with which I see God is the same with which God sees me."

IRA PROGOFF

July 1957
New York

TABLE OF THE CHAPTERS

The Cloud of Unknowing

43

THE CLOUD OF UNKNOWING

Classic Text

THE PRAYER OF THE PROLOGUE

God unto whom all hearts are open and unto whom every will speaks, and from whom no secret thing is hidden, I pray Thee to cleanse the intent of my heart with the ineffable gift of Thy grace, that I may perfectly love Thee, and worthily praise Thee. Amen.

PROLOGUE

1. In the name of the Father and the Son and of the Holy Ghost. I charge you and I beseech you with as much power and strength as the bond of charity will permit, that whoever you may be who comes into possession of this book, whether as your own property or by borrowing, that you neither read it nor write it nor permit it to be read, written, or spoken by any one who has not as far as you can judge a full desire and intention to be a perfect follower of Christ not only in his active life but in the ultimate degree of contemplation to which it is possible to attain by grace in this life by a perfect soul still dwelling in a mortal body; and if you know that he does those things and has done so for a long time before, so that he has become capable of contemplative living by the virtuous means of active life, you may permit him to read this book. Otherwise, it is not for him.

2. And in addition to this, I charge you and I beseech you by the authority of charity that if any such person shall read it, write it, or speak it, or shall hear it be read or spoken, that you shall charge him as I now do you to take his time in reading it, speaking it, writing it, or hearing

it, and above all to consider it as a whole. For it may be that there is some subject in the beginning or in the middle that is left hanging, unclear and still unresolved with no clear statement of where it belongs. But if there is no such statement there, there will be one soon afterward, or else it will appear before the end. On this score, if a man saw one subject and not another, he might easily be led into error; and in order that such an error may be avoided, both in yourself and in all others who may come to this book, I earnestly pray that you do as I request of you, for the sake of charity.

3. Sensual men who babble compliments and criticize both themselves and others, all tellers of tales, whisperers of trifles and covetous persons, I would prefer that they never saw this book. My intention was not at all to write such a book for them, and I hope that they will not meddle with it, neither they nor the idly curious, whether they be learned men or not. Even though they may be very good and virtuous men in their daily life, this subject is of no relevance for them.

4. If, on the other hand, this book should come to those men who follow the activities of an outward life, but who are drawn nonetheless by an inward stirring toward the secret spirit of God whose judgments are hidden, it is good that they read the book if they are disposed to do so. They should not read it continually as is proper for men who are living the full contemplative life; but they should read it now and then, so that they too may be perceivers of this highest point of the contemplative act. If such men

see it, they should by the grace of God be highly comforted by it.

5. This book is divided into seventy-five chapters, and of these, the last chapter discloses certain signs by which a soul may determine whether or not he has been called by God to practice this work.

CHAPTER I

Of the Four degrees of Christian living
and the purpose for which this book
was written

1. SPIRITUAL FRIEND IN GOD, understand well that I find by general observation four degrees and forms of Christian living. These are called: Common; Special; Singular; and Perfect. The first three of these may be begun and ended in this life. The fourth may be begun here by grace, and it shall continue without end in the bliss of heaven. Just as you see the order they are set in here one after the other, Common, Special, Singular, and Perfect, so it seems to me that the Lord in His great mercy has called you and led you to Him out of the desire of your heart in this same order and by the same degrees.

2. FROM THE FIRST you knew well, as it seems to me, that when you were living in the common degree of Christian life in company with your worldly friends that the everlasting love of His Godhead, through which He created you and formed you when you were nothing and has since bought you with the price of His precious blood

when you were lost in Adam, would not permit you to remain so far from Him in form and degree of living. Therefore he kindled your desire with the greatest grace and attached to it a leash of longing, and led you by it into a more special state and form of living, to be a servant among His special servants, where you might learn to live more excellently and more spiritually in His service than you did or than you might have done in the common degree of living before. And how much more besides?

3. IT SEEMS, nevertheless, that He would not leave you so easily, because of the love of His heart which He has forever possessed for you since you were created. What did He then? Do you not see with what great care and favor He has secretly drawn you to the third degree, the third manner of living which is called Singular? In this solitary form and manner of living, you may learn to lift up the foot of your love, and you may step toward that state and degree of living that is the perfect one, the last state of all.

CHAPTER II

A short stirring to meekness and to the
work of this book

1. LOOK UP NOW, weak and wretched man, and see what
you are. What are you, and what have you done to deserve
to be called by the Lord? What weary wretched heart
asleep in laziness can help but be wakened by the draught
of this love and the voice of this calling! Beware of this,
wretched man, while you are still engaged with your
enemy. And do not esteem yourself as holier or better
because of the high worth of this calling and because of
the singular form of living in which you now are.

2. YOU SHALL BE, indeed, all the more wretched and
accursed unless you live according to your calling by grace
and by learning. You should be ever more meek and loving
toward your spiritual spouse who is the Almighty God,
the King of Kings and the Lord of Lords. For He has
made Himself so humble before you and before all the
flock of His sheep as to choose you graciously to be one
of His special ones, and accordingly set you in the place
of pasture where you may be fed with the sweetness of

His love while you earnestly seek your heritage, the Kingdom of Heaven.

3. Go FORWARD then steadfastly. Look forward, and do not be concerned with things that are behind you. Consider what you lack and not what you already possess for that is the best way to acquire meekness, to find it and to keep it. And now it is necessary that all your life be brought completely to one desire, if you are to advance in the degree of your perfection. This desire is to be formed within your will, by the hand of Almighty God and with your consent.

4. BUT this one thing I must tell you. He is a jealous lover and He will not be part of a fellowship. Unless He alone is with you, He will not bother to work in your will. He asks none to help Him, but only you. He wishes only that you turn your attention to Him, and then let Him alone. You must only guard the windows and doors for flies and enemies who may intrude. And if you willingly do only this, then you will need only to speak quietly and humbly in prayer and soon He will help you. Go forward then, and let us see how you carry yourself. He is ready and He is waiting for you. But what will you do? And how will you go forward?

CHAPTER III

How the work of this book is to be
carried out and its value beyond all
other works

1. LIFT UP YOUR HEART TO GOD with a meek stirring of
love, seeking God Himself and none of His created things.
Think of nothing but God Himself, so that nothing will
work in your mind, or in your will, but only God Himself.
You must then do whatever will help you forget all the
beings whom God has created and all their works. Your
thoughts and your desires are not to be directed toward
them nor to touch them in any way, neither in general,
nor in any particular case; but you are to let them be and
pay no attention to them.

2. THIS IS THE WORK OF THE SOUL that is most pleasing
to God. All the saints and angels rejoice in this work and
they do all that is in their power to assist it. By contrast,
all the demons will be furious at your doing this work,
and they will try to defeat it in every way they can. All
of mankind living on earth will be helped by this work in
wonderful ways of which you are not even aware.

3. IN FACT, even the souls in purgatory will be eased in their pain because of this work. And you yourself are cleansed and made virtuous by no other work as much as by this. And yet this is the simplest work of all, the easiest and the speediest to accomplish, if the soul is only helped by the grace of feeling a strong desire to do it. Otherwise it is hard, and it is a marvel if you do it.

4. DO NOT SLACKEN, therefore, but persevere in the work until you feel the desire. For, when you begin it, you will find that there is at the start but a darkness; there is, as it were, a cloud of unknowing. You know not what it is except that you feel in your will a naked intent toward God.

5. NO MATTER WHAT YOU DO, this darkness and this cloud is between you and your God and because of it you can neither see Him clearly with your reason in the light of understanding, nor can you feel Him with your affection in the sweetness of love. Be prepared, therefore, to remain in this darkness as long as must be, crying evermore for Him whom you love. For if you are ever to feel Him or to see Him, it will necessarily be within this cloud and within this darkness. And if you will work with great effort as I bid you, I trust in His mercy that you will achieve it.

CHAPTER IV

On the brevity of this work and how it is not to be achieved by curiosity of mind nor by imagination

1. In order that you do not err in this work and misconceive it to be something other than it is, I will tell you a little more about it as it seems to me.

2. To do this work properly does not require a long time as some men believe; it is the shortest work that man can imagine. It is neither longer nor shorter than an atom; and an atom is by the definition of true philosophers in the science of astronomy the least part of time. It is so small, in fact, that it is indivisible and practically incomprehensible.

3. It is this time of which it has been written: of the time that has been given to you, you shall be asked how you have spent it. And it is certainly reasonable that you give an account of it; for it is neither longer nor shorter, but varies according to only one stirring within the principal working power of your soul, namely, your will.

4. THERE CAN BE just so many willings or desirings, no more and no fewer, may be and are in one hour in your will as there are atoms in one hour. And if you were transformed by grace to the primary state of man's soul as it was before sin, you would forever afterwards by means of that grace be master of that stirring or of those stirrings. None would then be lost, but they would all stretch to the ultimate desirable, the highest willable thing, which is God.

5. HE ACCORDS WITH OUR SOUL in terms of the limits of His Godhead; and our soul accords to Him because of the high worth of our having been created in His image and in His likeness. And He by Himself alone is more than sufficient to fulfill the will and desire of our soul; and none but He may do so. Our soul by virtue of this transforming grace then becomes altogether capable of comprehending God by love; and this, like knowing an angel or a man's soul, is beyond the comprehension of all man's created powers of knowledge. I mean by knowing and not by loving, and that is why I refer to them here as powers of knowledge, with another main effective power referred to as the loving power.

6. WITH RESPECT TO THESE POWERS, God is the creator of them. The first is the power of knowledge, and to this God is incomprehensible. The second is the loving power, and by means of this, God may be comprehended fully by each person, but by each in a different way. To the extent that a loving soul alone by virtue of its love should comprehend Him within itself all the souls and

angels that ever may be are filled to the full, and much more still, beyond comparison. This is the infinite and marvelous miracle of life whose effects go on without end; forever shall He do it, and He shall never cease doing it. Whoever has the grace to see this, see it; for the feeling of this is endless bliss, and the contrary is endless pain.

7. For this reason, whoever has been transformed by grace so that he follows this way of obeying the urgings of his will should not remain in this life without some taste of the infinite sweetness; for, just as he is not without these urgings in nature, so he may not be in the bliss of heaven without the full food.

8. Do not wonder, therefore, that I urge you on to this work. For this is a work, as you shall learn in a little while, that man would have continued to do if he had never sinned. And it was for this work that man was made, as all things also were made to help him and further him in this work, so that by means of it man shall be made whole again. And by failing to carry out this work, a man falls ever deeper and deeper into sin and is drawn ever further and further away from God. But by holding to this work and working in it continually, a man rises ever higher and higher away from sin and comes closer and closer to God.

9. Pay close attention to time, therefore, and consider how you spend it; for nothing is more precious than time. In one little moment, as small as it may be, heaven may be won or lost. Here is a token of the fact that time is precious: God, who is the giver of time, never

gives two moments together, but only separately, each one after the other. He does this because He does not wish to reverse the ordered course of His creation.

10. TIME WAS MADE FOR MAN, and not man for time; and therefore, God, who is the ruler of nature, will not, as He gives time to man, go beyond the urges of nature in man's soul, for these occur only one moment at a time. Because of this, man cannot have the excuse when he comes before God on the Day of Judgment to give an account of how he has spent his time, to say, "Thou hast given me two moments at once, and I have but one urge at once."

11. BUT SORROWFULLY you now say, "What shall I do? How shall I give an account of each moment separately in the terms that you have spoken? Until today when I am twenty-four years of age, I never paid any attention to time. If I were to change now, you know very well because of things that you yourself have already written, that it might very well be neither according to the course of nature nor of common grace for me to pay attention and act satisfactorily any more times in the future than in the past. And moreover, I am quite certain that of those times that are to come in the future, my weakness and slowness of spirit will prevent me from observing more than one in a hundred. For these reasons I am truly caught and shut in. Help me now for the love of Jesus."

12. YOU HAVE SPOKEN WELL in saying, "For the love of Jesus." It is from the love of Jesus that your help shall

come. Love is such a power that it unites all things. Therefore love Jesus, and then everything that He has will be yours. He by virtue of His Godhead is the maker and the giver of time. He by virtue of His manhood is the very keeper of time. And He, by virtue of His Godhead and His manhood together, is the ultimate judge, the ultimate one to demand an accounting of how one's time has been spent. Bind yourself to Him, therefore, by love and by belief; and by virtue of the knot that binds you, you shall perceive together with Him and with all who are likewise bound to Him by love; that is to say, with our Lady Saint Mary who possessed the highest grace in the keeping of time, and with all the saints in heaven and on earth who, by the grace of Jesus, take heed of time properly in terms of love.

13. IN THIS LIES TRUE CONSOLATION. Understand what is worth-while. You must be warned, however, of one thing more than all other. No one can truly claim community with this Jesus and His good mother, His high angels, and His saints, if he is not a person who does everything he can in making use of time with the help of grace. He will then be seen to be one who uses his time to advantage in improving himself, and making his contribution to the community, as much as that may be, on the same terms as each of the others offers of himself.

14. PAY ATTENTION TO THIS WORK, therefore, and to its marvelous ways within your soul. When it has been truly conceived, it comes merely as a sudden stirring with no forewarning, instantly springing toward God as a spark

from a coal. And it is wonderful to count the number of stirrings that may appear within one hour in a soul that is disposed to the work.

15. AND YET, in any one of these stirrings every created thing may suddenly and completely be forgotten. But immediately after each stirring, because of the corruption of the flesh, it drops down again to some thought or to some deed that has been or has not been committed. And what follows? Immediately it rises just as suddenly as it had done before.

16. FROM THIS, it may be seen in brief what the manner of this working actually is, so that man can clearly know that it is far indeed from being a fantasy or a false imagination or a quaint opinion; for these latter do not arise from such a devout humility and a blind stirring of love, but are the result of a proud, curious, and imaginative mind. Such a proud and curious mind must always be borne down and sternly trodden under foot, if this work is conceived in full purity of spirit.

17. IF THERE IS ANYONE who either hears this work being read or spoken of and thinks that it can be comprehended by working with his mind so that he sits and seeks with his mind to know how and what it may be; and if, in his curiosity he uses his imagination perhaps against the course of nature and pretends to a manner of working which is neither physical nor spiritual—truly, such a man, whoever he may be, is dangerously deceived. In fact, if God in His great goodness does not soon show him a

miracle of mercy to cause him to leave off his work and become humble enough to take counsel from proved workers, he will soon fall either into frenzies or into other great mischiefs that are spiritual sins and devil's deceptions; and through these, he may easily lose both his body and his soul eternally. Therefore, for the love of God, be careful in this work and do not by any means work in it with your mind or with your imagination; for I tell you, it cannot be achieved by working with them, and therefore leave them alone and do not work with them.

18. AND DO NOT BELIEVE that because I call it a darkness or a cloud that it is a cloud formed out of the moisture in the air, nor that it is the kind of darkness that is in your house at night when the candle is out. That kind of darkness or that kind of cloud you can imagine merely out of the curiosity of your mind, and you can carry it before your eyes in the brightest day of summer, just as you can imagine a clear and shining light on the darkest night of winter. Leave such falsehoods alone. They are not what I am talking about. When I speak of darkness, I am referring to a lack of knowing. It is a lack of knowing that includes everything you do not know or else that you have forgotten, whatever is altogether dark for you because you do not see it with your spiritual eye. And for this reason it is not called a cloud of the air, but rather a cloud of unknowing that is between you and your God.

CHAPTER V

That when this work is being done, all
the creatures that ever have been, are, or
ever will be, and all their works shall be
hidden beneath the cloud of unknowing

1. AND IF EVER you come to this cloud to dwell in it
and work in it as I bid you, then, just as this cloud of
unknowing is above you and between you and your God,
it will be necessary for you to put in the same way a
cloud of forgetting beneath you, between you and all the
creatures that have ever been made. You may think,
perhaps, that you are very far from God because this
cloud of unknowing is between you and your God. That
may well be true, but you are certainly much farther
from Him when you do not have a cloud of forgetting
between you and all the creatures that have ever been
made. And when I say all the creatures that have ever
been made I mean not only the creatures themselves but
also all the works and the conditions of these creatures,
whether they be good or evil. And briefly I say that all
should be hid beneath the cloud of unknowing.

2. EVEN THOUGH it may be quite worth-while to think of certain conditions and deeds of some special creatures, nevertheless in this work it is of very little help, or none at all. Why is this so? Memory or thought concerning any creature that God has made, or of any of their deeds, is a kind of spiritual light; for the eye of your soul opens upon it and becomes fixed upon it, as the eye of the archer is fixed on the spot at which he aims. And one thing I tell you, that whatever you think about is above you for a time and is between you and your God. And to the extent that anything is in your mind other than God, you are that much further from God.

3. INDEED, if it will be considered courteous and proper to say so, it is of very little value or of no value at all in this work to think about the kindness or the great worth of God, nor of our Lady, nor of the saints or angels in heaven, nor even of the joys in heaven. It is of no value, that is to say, to hold them intently before your mind as you would do in order to strengthen and increase your purpose. I believe that it would not be helpful at all in accomplishing this work. For, even though it is good to think about the kindness of God, and to love Him and to praise Him for it, nevertheless it is far better to think about His naked being and to praise him and to love Him for Himself.

CHAPTER VI

A short statement of the work of this book treated by question

1. BUT NOW you put a question to me asking, "How shall I think about Him, and what is He?" And to this I can only answer you, "I do not know."

2. WITH YOUR QUESTION you have brought me into that same darkness and into that same cloud of unknowing into which I would wish you to be in yourself. Through grace a man can have great knowledge of all other creatures and their works, and even of the works of God Himself, and he can think of them all; but of God Himself no man can think. I would therefore leave all those things of which I can think and choose for my love that thing of which I cannot think.

3. AND WHY IS THIS SO? He may be well loved, but he may not be thought of. He may be reached and held close by means of love, but by means of thought never. And therefore, even though it is good occasionally to think of the kindness and the great worth of God in particular

aspects, and even though it is a joy that is a proper part of contemplation, nevertheless in this work it should be cast down and covered with a cloud of forgetting.

4. YOU ARE TO STEP ABOVE IT with great courage and with determination, and with a devout and pleasant stirring of love, and you are to try to pierce that darkness which is above you. You are to strike that thick cloud of unknowing with a sharp dart of longing love; and you are not to retreat no matter what comes to pass.

CHAPTER VII

How a man in this work is to turn himself against all thoughts and particularly
those that arise out of his own knowledge and natural mind

1. AND IF A THOUGHT SHOULD ARISE and insert itself
continually above you, between you and that darkness,
and if it should ask you, "What are you seeking and what
do you wish to have?" you are to answer that it is God
that you wish to have. "Him I covet, Him I seek, and
nothing but Him."

2. AND IF HE* SHOULD ASK YOU, "What is that
God?" you are to answer that it is God who made you
and formed you and has graciously called you to your
present degree. "And in Him," you are to reply, "you

* [Occasionally the text uses the pronoun "he" to refer to an object
that would ordinarily be spoken of as "it" in modern speech. Here the
reference is to a thought, and the meaning of the text is best rendered
by "he" both because it conveys the active and independent quality of
thoughts that rise in the mind and because the author of *The Cloud of
Unknowing* identifies these thoughts with the "tempter" or antagonist
of God. I.P.]

have no skill." And then you are to say, "Get down again," and you are to tread him down again firmly with a stirring of love, even though he may seem to you to be quite a holy thought that might even be of help to you in seeking God.

3. IT MAY BE that he will bring to your mind a great many excellent and wonderful points regarding God's kindness, saying that God is exceedingly tender, full of love and graciousness and mercy. And he wants nothing more than for you to listen to him. And then he will chatter on more and more until, as he brings you lower and lower, he will eventually bring you down to the remembrance of His Passion.

4. ONCE THERE, he will let you see a wonderful kindness of God, and if you will listen to him he wants nothing better. For soon afterward he will let you see your wretched life of the past and perhaps while you are seeing it and thinking of it he will bring to your mind some place where you have lived before this time. Then you will feel yourself to be scattered you know not where. The reason for this scattering will be that at the beginning you listened to him willfully, then answered him, received him, and did not harm him.

5. DESPITE THIS, the things he said were both good and holy. In fact, they were exceedingly holy, for any man or woman who believed that he could come to contemplation without first having had many meditations on his own wretchedness as well as upon the passion, the

kindness, and the great goodness and worth of God would surely be in error and would fail to achieve his purpose. And yet, even though this is true, it is necessary for a man or woman who has been engaged in these meditations for a long time to discontinue them all the same and to press them down and hold them far down beneath the cloud of forgetting if he is ever to pierce the cloud of unknowing that is between him and his God.

6. FOR THIS REASON, whenever you feel yourself drawn to devote yourself to this work, and whenever you feel by grace that you have been called by God to do it, lift up your heart toward God with a meek stirring of love. And understand by God the God who made you and formed you and who has graciously called you to your present degree; and do not accept in your mind any other conception of God. And not even all of this is necessary, but only if you are so inclined; for a naked intent direct to God is sufficient without anything else.

7. AND IF YOU DESIRE to have this aim concentrated and expressed in one word in order that you may be better able to grasp it, take but one short word of a single syllable. This is better than two, for the shorter it is the better it accords with the work of the spirit. Such a word is the word GOD or the word LOVE. Choose whichever one you prefer, or, if you like, choose another that suits your taste, provided that it is of one syllable. And clasp this word tightly in your heart so that it never leaves it no matter what may happen.

8. THIS WORD shall be your shield and your spear whether you ride in peace or in war. With this word you shall beat upon the cloud and the darkness, which are above you. With this word you shall strike down thoughts of every kind and drive them beneath the cloud of forgetting.

9. AFTER THAT, if any thought should press upon you to ask you what you are seeking, answer him with this word only and with no other words. And if he should offer you his great learning and offer to expound that word for you and to tell you all the conditions and modifications of that word, you are to answer him that you will have it whole and not broken apart or analyzed. And if you will hold fast to this purpose, you can be sure that he will not remain very long. And why is this so? Because you will then not let him feed himself on such sweet meditations of God as we described before.

CHAPTER VIII

A good statement of certain doubts that
may occur during this work, treated by
question, with respect to overcoming a
man's curiosity and cunning and natural
mind and distinguishing the degrees and
parts of active and contemplative life

1. Now YOU ASK ME, "What is he that thus presses
upon me in this work? Is it a good thing or an evil thing?
And if it is an evil thing, must we not wonder at the
fact that he increases a man's devotion so much? For sometimes it seems to me to be exceedingly pleasant to listen
to his tales. One moment he makes me weep with the
fullest pity of my heart for the Passion of Christ, and
another moment for my own wretchedness and then for
many other reasons so that it seems to me to be exceedingly holy and to have done me much good. For this reason
it seems to me that he can in no sense be evil. And if
he is good and if in addition he does me so much good
with his pleasant stories, then I do not understand why
you instruct me to press him down and away far beneath
the cloud of forgetting."

2. Now it certainly seems to me that this is a very good question, and I shall try to answer it as best I can. Firstly, when you ask what he is that presses so hard upon you in this work while offering to help you in it, I say that it is a sharp and clear perception of means of your natural capacities expressed in your reason within your soul. And when you ask me whether it is good or evil, I answer that it must always be good in its nature. The reason for this is that it is a beam of the image of God.

3. The use of it, however, may be both good and evil. It may be good when it is opened by grace in order to see the wretchedness, the passion, the kindness, and the wonderful works of God in His creatures both physical and spiritual. In that case it must certainly increase your devotion fully as much as you say.

4. On the other hand, its use is evil when it is swollen with pride and with the curiosity of much learning and literary cunning as in scholars, and when it makes them strive to be regarded not as meek scholars or masters of divinity or of devotion, but as proud scholars of the devil, and as masters of vanity and falsehood. In other men and women, whether they be religious or secular people, the use and working of this natural knowledge is evil when it is swollen with the proud and curious skills of worldly things and with sensual fancies coveting worldly fame and riches, vain pleasures, and the flattery of others.

5. Now as for your question where you ask me why they are to press it down beneath the cloud of for-

getting when it is good in its nature and does you so much good, even increasing your devotion when it is well used. In answer to this I say that there are two ways of living in the Holy Church. One is an active life; the other is a contemplative life.

6. THE ACTIVE LIFE is the lower one, and the contemplative life is the higher one. Active life has two degrees, a higher and a lower; and the contemplative life likewise has two degrees, a lower and a higher. Also these two lives are so joined together that neither of them may be had fully without some part of the other, although they are quite different in their respective parts.

7. WHY IS THIS SO? The reason is that the highest part of the active life is at the same time the lower part of the contemplative life. Because of this, a man cannot be considered to be living fully the active life unless he is living partly as a contemplative; and, correspondingly, a man is not living fully as a contemplative unless he lives partly an active life.

8. THE CONDITION OF THE ACTIVE LIFE is such that it both begins and ends in this life; but that is not the case with the contemplative life. It begins in this life, but it continues thereafter without end. Why is this so? The part that Mary chose shall never be taken away. Active life is full of troubles and worries concerning many things; but the contemplative person sits in peace with one thing.

9. THE LOWER PART OF ACTIVE LIFE consists in good

and honest bodily works of mercy and charity. The higher part of active life and the lower part of contemplative life consist in good spiritual meditations, the earnest observing of a man's own wretchedness with sorrow and contrition, considering the Passion of Christ and of His servants with pity and compassion, and considering with thanks and praise the wonderful gifts, the kindness and works of God in all His creatures physical and spiritual. But the higher part of the contemplative life, as it may be had here, takes place altogether in this darkness and in this cloud of unknowing with a loving stirring blindly beholding the naked being only of God Himself.

10. IN THE LOWER PART OF THE ACTIVE LIFE a man is without himself and beneath himself. In the higher part of the active life and in the lower part of the contemplative life, a man is within himself and even with himself. But in the higher part of the contemplative life, a man is above himself and under his God.

11. AND WHY IS IT that he is above himself? It is because he is seeking to attain by grace something that he cannot attain by his very nature, namely, to be knit to God in spirit, in unity of love, and accordance of will.

12. FURTHER, just as it is impossible, at least to our understanding, for a man to come to the higher part of the active life without first ceasing for a time to live on the lower part; so also a man cannot come to the higher part of the contemplative life unless he cease for a time living on the lower part.

13. FURTHER, just as it would be unlawful and would seriously hinder a man who was sitting in his meditations to turn his attention to his outward bodily works, whether they were those that he had done or those that he should do, no matter how holy the works might be in themselves; so also, unlikely a thing as that would be, so would it hinder a man undertaking to work in this darkness and in this cloud of unknowing with a passionate stirring of love to God for Himself, if he would let any thought or any meditation of God's wonderful gifts, kindness, and works in any of His creatures physical or spiritual rise upon him to press between him and his God, no matter how holy these thoughts might be, nor how profound, nor how pleasant.

14. THIS IS THE REASON for which I bid you put down such a sharp and subtle thought and cover him with a thick cloud of forgetting, no matter how holy he may be and no matter how much he may promise to help you in your purpose. And this is because love may reach God in this life, but not knowledge. And as long as the soul dwells in this mortal body the accuracy of our understanding in perceiving spiritual things, most particularly God, is mingled with some manner of fantasy that tends to make our work unclean. And, were it not for a greater marvel, it would lead us into much error.

CHAPTER IX

That when this work is being done
the remembrance of the holiest creature
that God ever made hinders more than
it helps

1. BECAUSE OF THIS, the sharp stirring of your understanding that will always press upon you when you set yourself to this work must always be borne down; and if you do not bear him down, he will bear you down. You will find, in this regard, that when your condition is such that you believe yourself best able to abide in darkness with nothing in your mind but only God, then if you look truly you will find that your mind is not occupied in this darkness but in a clear perceiving of something beneath God. And if this is so, then certainly this thing that is above you for the time is between you and your God.

2. BE DETERMINED, therefore, to press down such clear perceivings, no matter how holy or how proper they may seem. One thing I tell you: it is of greater value to the health of your soul, more worthy in itself, and more pleasing to God and to all the saints and angels in heaven—

yes, and more helpful to all your friends, physical and spiritual, living and dead—when you have such a blind stirring of love unto God for Himself and such a secret pressing upon this cloud of unknowing. It is better for you to have this and to feel it in your spiritual desires than it is for you to have the eyes of your soul opened in contemplation or in the perceiving of all the angels or saints in heaven, or in hearing all the mirth and melody they possess in bliss.

3. YOU SHOULD NOT MARVEL at this. If you would once see it as clearly as you may come by grace to touch it and feel it in this life, you would agree with what I say. But you may be sure that man will never have clear sight here in this life, although men may have the feeling through grace when God permits it. Therefore lift up your love to that cloud; or rather, if I would speak it to you truly, let God draw your love up to that cloud and then strive with the help of God's grace to forget every other thing.

4. CONSIDERING THAT the mere remembrance of any-thing under God pressing against your will and against your awareness draws you farther from God than you would be if it were not there; and considering that it hinders you, and makes you that much less able to feel an actual experience of the fruit of His love; how much, do you think, a remembrance that you knowingly and delib-erately draw upon yourself will hold you back from your purpose? And considering, too, that a remembrance of any special saint or of any pure spiritual thing will hold you back so much, how much do you think that the remem-

brance of any man living in this wretched life, or any other bodily or worldly thing, will hinder you in this work?

5. I AM NOT SAYING that such a pure and spontaneous thought, any clean and good spiritual thing under God, pressing against your will or your awareness, or else deliberately drawn to yourself with the aim of increasing your devotion, is necessarily evil, even though it is a hindrance in this type of work. No, God forbid that you take it so! But I do say that even though it may be good and holy, it will nevertheless hinder more than it helps in this work. I mean at least temporarily; for certainly he who is seeking God perfectly will not be finally content with the remembrance of any angel or saint that is in heaven.

CHAPTER X

How a man shall know when his
thought is not a sin, and if so, when it
is mortal, and when it is venial

1. IT IS NOT THE SAME, however, for the remembrance of any man or woman living in this life, or for bodily or worldly things of any kind. When a simple thought of any of them suddenly presses against your will and against your consciousness—although certainly no sin is to be imputed to you because of it, for it is the pain of the original sin of which you were cleansed by baptism—nevertheless, if this sudden stirring or thought is not immediately pressed down it reaches the weakness of your fleshly heart. It does this either with some form of delight, if it is a thing that pleases you or has pleased you in the past; or with something that causes you to complain if it is something that grieves you, or has grieved you before.

2. THIS ATTACHMENT may be mortal for men or women living carnally who have been in mortal sin before; but for you and all others like you who have forsaken the world with a true will and who have taken a vow either

secretly or openly for any degree of devout living in the Holy Church, and who accordingly are governed not by their own wills nor by their own powers of knowledge but by the advice of their masters whether religious or secular, for all such it is only a venial sin. The reason for this is the grounding and the rooting of your intent in God made at the beginning of your life in the state that you are in, witnessed by some discreet father and with his advice.

3. IF THIS PLEASURE or this complaint that has found a place in your fleshly heart is permitted to remain with nothing done to alter it, it eventually becomes attached to your spiritual heart, that is to say, to your will with your full consent. Then it becomes a mortal sin. This comes to pass when you, or any of those of whom I speak, deliberately draw to yourselves the remembrance of any man or woman living in this life, or of any other bodily or worldly thing. If it is something that grieves you or has grieved you in the past, it will arouse in you an angry passion and a desire for vengeance; and this is called Wrath. Or else it will arouse a cruel disdain with a feeling of loathesomeness for their person with spiteful and condemning thoughts; and this is called Envy. Or else it will bring a weariness and a lack of desire for any good occupation whether physical or spiritual; and this is called Sloth.

4. IF, ON THE OTHER HAND, it is a thing that pleases you or that has pleased you in the past, there will arise in you a strong delight when thinking about that thing, whatever

it may be. If you remain with that thought and eventually fasten your heart and your will to it, and if you feed your fleshly heart with it so that you feel at that moment that you desire nothing else but to live in tranquillity with the thing of which you are thinking; and if this thought that you draw in this way upon yourself or that you receive when it is brought to you and hold with pleasure, if this thought concerns the great worth of your nature, or your knowledge, or your grace or degree, or your beauty in appearance, then it is Pride. And if the thought is of any kind of worldly goods, riches, or chattels, or whatever a man may possess and rule over, then it is Covetousness. And if the thought is of fine meats and drinks, or any kind of delight that a man may taste, then it is Gluttony. And if the thought is of love or of merriment, or of any kind of carnal caressing, fondling, or flattering of any man or woman living in this life, or of yourself either, then it is Lust.

CHAPTER XI

That a man should weigh each thought
and each stirring according to its nature
and not be careless as to venial sin

1. I AM NOT SAYING these things because I think that you or any other people of whom I am speaking are guilty of or are encumbered with such sins; but I say it so that you will weigh each thought and each stirring according to what it truly is. My wish is that you strive with the greatest effort to destroy the very first stirring and thought of those things in which you might possibly sin.

2. ONE THING I tell you: whoever fails to consider the first thought that comes to him—even though it is not a sin in him—or whoever considers it to be of little importance will not avoid venial sin. No man can completely avoid venial sin in this mortal life. But carelessness with regard to venial sin should always be avoided by all true disciples of perfection. Otherwise I have no doubt but that they would soon commit a mortal sin.

CHAPTER XII

That this work not only destroys sin but engenders virtue

1. IF YOU WISH to stand and not fall, therefore, never slack in your purpose, but beat constantly with a sharp dart of longing love upon this cloud of unknowing which is between you and your God. As you do this, do not think of anything under God, and do not let up no matter what happens. For this is the work that destroys the ground and root of sin.

2. NO MATTER HOW MUCH you may fast; no matter how long you stay awake; no matter how early you arise; no matter how hard your bed and how unpleasant your clothes. Indeed—if it were permitted to do so, as it is not— no matter if you put out your eyes, cut your tongue out of your mouth, stopped up your ears and your nose, cut off your limbs, and inflicted upon your body every pain of which you can possibly conceive—all of this would help you not at all. The stirring and rising of sin would still be in you.

3. YES, AND WHAT FURTHER? No matter how much you may weep because of your sorrow for your sins, or for the Passion of Christ. No matter how much you may think of the joys of heaven. What will that do for you? Surely it will bring you much good, much help, much profit, and much grace; but what it does is very little when compared with what may be accomplished by the blind stirring of love. This by itself and without anything else is the best part of Mary. Those who are without it gain little or nothing. It not only destroys the ground and root of sin as it may be here, but it brings additional virtues. When it is truly understood, all virtues are fully and perfectly felt and comprehended within it and no impure intentions spoil it from without. For no matter how many virtues a man may have without it they are always mingled with some dishonest intention that makes them dishonest.

4. VIRTUE IS NOTHING ELSE but a definite and measured desire plainly directed toward God for Himself, for God in Himself is the pure cause of all virtues. If a man is stirred to a virtue by any cause mixed together with God, even though God may be the chief cause, that virtue is imperfect. We can see in the example of one or two virtues what is contained in all the others. Especially is this true of the two virtues of meekness and charity. Whoever possesses these two clearly needs no more. He has all.

CHAPTER XIII

What meekness is in itself and when
it is perfect and when imperfect

1. LET US NOW CONSIDER the quality of meekness when it is imperfect, when it is imperfect by virtue of being caused by something in addition to God, even though God may be the chief cause; and after that, let us consider it when it is perfect by virtue of having been caused by God Himself. The first question is what meekness is in itself, if this matter can clearly be seen and conceived. From that we can conceive more accurately in truth of spirit what the cause is.

2. MEEKNESS IN ITSELF is nothing else than a true knowing and feeling of a man's self as he is. Any man who truly sees and feels himself as he is must surely be meek indeed. This meekness has two causes. One is the filth, the wretchedness, and the frailty of man into which he has fallen by sin, and which he must always feel in some degree as long as he lives in this life no matter how holy he is. The other is the overabundant love and worth of God in Himself, for in beholding this all nature quakes,

all scholars are fools, and all saints and angels are blind. In fact, if it were not that through the wisdom of His Godhead he had judged their beholding of Him according to their ability in nature and in grace, I cannot say what would happen to them.

3. THIS LATTER CAUSE is perfect, for it shall last without end. The former, however, is imperfect, for it not only fails at the end of this life, but very often it happens that because of an abundance of grace in multiplying his desires —as often and as long as God makes it possible—a soul in this mortal body suddenly and completely loses and forgets all awareness and feeling of his being and no longer cares whether he is holy or wretched.

4. WHETHER THIS HAPPENS OFTEN or seldom to a soul who is so disposed, I believe that it lasts only for a very short while. In this time the soul is made altogether humble, for it knows and feels no cause but the Chief One. And if it knows and feels the other cause, even though God remains the chief cause, it is still imperfect meekness. Nevertheless, this is good and is necessary; and God forbid that you take this in any other manner than I say.

CHAPTER XIV

Unless imperfect meekness comes first,
it is impossible for a sinner to reach the
perfect virtue of meekness in this life

1. EVEN THOUGH I call it imperfect meekness, I would much rather have a true knowledge of myself as I am, for I believe that this would achieve for me the perfect type and quality of meekness by itself much sooner than if all the saints and angels in heaven and all the men and women of the Holy Church living on earth, religious or secular ones of all degrees, would come together all at once and do nothing else than pray to God for me to achieve perfect meekness. In fact, without this it is impossible for a sinner to achieve, or to keep once he has achieved, the perfect quality of meekness.

2. LABOR AND SWEAT, therefore, in every way that you can, seeking to obtain for yourself a true knowledge and feeling of yourself as you are; and then I believe that soon afterward you will have a true knowledge and feeling of God as He is. Not as He is in Himself, for no man can achieve that, but only God Himself. Neither shall you

know Him as you shall in the bliss of Heaven with both your body and soul. But you shall know Him to the extent that it is possible and in the way that He permits Himself to be known and felt by a humble soul living in this mortal body.

3. Do NOT THINK that because I distinguish two types of meekness, one perfect and the other imperfect, that I therefore want you to stop working for imperfect meekness and to seek perfect meekness altogether. Certainly not; I believe that you would never be able to achieve it. That is why I will do what I am now about to do.

4. I NOW PROPOSE to tell you and to let you see the great worth of this spiritual exercise beyond all other exercises physical or spiritual that man can or may do by grace: how a secret love pressed in purity of spirit upon this dark cloud of unknowing between you and your God truly and perfectly contains within it the perfect quality of meekness without any special or clear beholding of any thing under God. I will do this because I desire you to know what perfect meekness is so that you can set it as a signpost before the love of your heart and perform it for yourself and for me; and because I wish by this knowledge to make you more humble.

5. IT OFTEN HAPPENS, so it seems to me, that the lack of knowledge is the cause of a great deal of pride. It might be, perhaps, that if you did not know what perfect meekness is you would think, when you had achieved a small knowledge and feeling of what I call imperfect meekness,

that you had almost reached perfect meekness. Then you would be deceiving yourself, believing that you were exceedingly humble when you were covered over with foul stinking pride. Try, therefore, to work for perfect meekness, for the condition of it is such that whoever has it commits no sin while he has it, and very little afterward.

CHAPTER XV

A short proof correcting those who say
that the main reason for humility is the
knowledge of man's own wretchedness

1. TRUST STEADFASTLY that there is such a perfect humility as I speak of, and that it may be achieved through grace in this life. I say this to refute those who state that the most perfect type of meekness is that which arises from the remembrance of our wretchedness and of the sins we have committed in the past.

2. I CONCEDE ALTOGETHER that for those people who have been living in accustomed sins, as I myself am and have been, it is most necessary and advantageous to become meek by means of the remembrance of our wretchedness and our past sins until such time as the great rust of sin will have been rubbed away as witnessed both by our consciousness and our spiritual director. But in the case of others who are, as it were, innocents who have never committed a mortal sin with a definite and deliberate will but only through weakness and lack of knowledge and who have become contemplatives; and in the case of ourselves

when both our spiritual director and our own consciousness attest to our having done proper penance in contrition
and in confession according to the statute and ordinance
of the all-Holy Church so that we feel stirred and called
by grace to be contemplatives as well, there is another
means of becoming humble.

3. THIS WAY of being made humble is as far superior to
the remembrance of our wretchedness and our past sins as
the life of our Lady Saint Mary is above the life of the
most sinful penitent in the Holy Church, or as the Life of
Christ is above the life of any man; or as the life of an
angel in heaven who has never felt and who never shall
feel human frailty is above the life of the weakest man
that is here in the world.

4. IF IT WERE TRUE that there is no perfect means by
which to be made humble except by seeing and feeling
one's own wretchedness, I would agree with those who
say that the nature of their meekness is such that they
neither see nor feel wretchedness nor stirring of sin, and
that they never have these within themselves. That is the
case with our Lord Jesus Christ, our Lady Saint Mary, and
all the saints and angels in heaven. Our Lord Jesus Christ
Himself called us to this and all other kinds of perfection
when he commanded us to be perfect by grace as He Himself is by nature.

CHAPTER XVI

That a sinner truly turned and called to
contemplation reaches perfection sooner
by this than by any other work and
receives God's forgiveness for his sins

1. WHEN A MAN has made the prescribed penance and
has felt himself called to that life which is called contemplative, and when he has received the assent both of
spiritual director and his conscience, he should by no
means consider it a presumptuous act for him to dare to
take it upon himself to offer a meek stirring of love to his
God, secretly pressing upon the cloud of unknowing that
is between him and his God. When our Lord spoke to
Mary as representative of all sinners who are called to the
contemplative life and said, "Thy sins be forgiven thee,"
it was not only because of her great sorrow, nor because
of her remembering her sins, nor even because of the
meekness with which she regarded her sinfulness. Why
then? It was surely because she loved much.

2. MEN MAY SEE from this what a secret pressing of love
may secure from our Lord, beyond all other works of

which man may conceive. I admit that she had a great deal of sorrow, that she wept very bitterly for her sins, and that she was made exceedingly humble by the remembrance of her sinfulness. And we also should do the same, we who have been wretched and habitual sinners. We too should make awful and wonderful sorrow for our sins and become exceedingly humble in remembering our wretchedness.

3. BUT HOW? Surely as Mary did. Even though she may not have felt a deep and strong sorrow for her sins—all her life she had them wherever she went as a burden bound together and placed secretly in the hole of her heart in a manner never to be forgotten—nevertheless it may be said and affirmed by Scripture that she had a stronger sorrow, a more doleful desire, and a deeper sadness; and she languished more for lack of love than for any remembrance of her sins. Yes, she languished almost to the death for lack of love even though she had a great deal of love. Do not wonder at this, for it is the condition of a true lover that the more he loves the more he longs to love.

4. SHE KNEW WELL and felt strongly in herself with a sad steadfastness that she was a wretch more foul than any other and that her sins had made a division between her and her God whom she loved so much. She knew also that they were in great part the cause of her languishing sickness for lack of love. But what followed? Did she therefore come down from the height of desire into the depths of her sinful life and search in the foul stinking fen and dunghill of her sins, searching them out one by one

with all their circumstances, sorrowing and weeping over each one? No, she certainly did not do this. And why not? Because God in His grace had permitted her to know within her soul that she could never achieve it in that way. Had she done that, she would more likely have developed in herself the ability to sin often than to have secured by that work the clear forgiveness for her sins.

5. INSTEAD, SHE HUNG UP HER LOVE and her longing desire in this cloud of unknowing and she learned to love a thing that she might never see clearly in this life, neither by the light of understanding of her reason nor by a true feeling of sweet love in her affection. Very often, in fact, she had hardly any special remembrance of whether she had been a sinner or not. Yes, and I hope that she was very often so deeply immersed in the love of His Godhead that she hardly saw the details of the beauty of His precious and His blessed body in which He sat speaking and preaching before her with such great love. Neither did she see anything else, neither physical nor spiritual. That this was the case is indicated by the gospel.

CHAPTER XVII

That a true contemplative does not
desire to mix in active life. He does not
care what is done or spoken about him,
and does not defend himself before his
critics

1. IN THE GOSPEL of Saint Luke it is written that when
our Lord was in the house of Martha, Mary, her sister,
sat at His feet all the time while Martha was busy preparing
His meat. And while Mary was listening to His word she
paid no attention to what her sister was doing although
that was very good and holy work, being truly the first
part of the active life. Neither did she pay attention to
the preciousness of His blessed body, nor to the sweet
voice and words of His manhood, although it would be
better and holier to do this since it is the second part of
the active life and the first part of the contemplative life.

2. BUT SHE DID PERCEIVE with all the love of her heart
the ultimate wisdom of His Godhead though it was covered over with the dark words of His manhood. Therefore

she would not move from where she was for anything that she saw or heard, or for anything that was being done around her. Rather, she sat in perfect stillness of body with the sweetest secret urgings of love pressing upon that high cloud of unknowing between her and her God.

3. THIS ONE THING I tell you, there has never yet been a pure creature in this life, nor shall there ever be one so completely transported by contemplation and the love of the Godhead that there will not still remain a large and wonderful cloud of unknowing between him and his God. It was in this cloud that Mary was occupied, pressed by many a secret love. And why was this so? Because it was the best and holiest part of contemplation that may be possible in this life, and from this she would not move her desire for anything. In fact, when her sister Martha complained about her to our Lord and asked Him to tell her to get up and help her so that she would not have to work so hard by herself, Mary remained sitting in perfect stillness, not answering a single word and not even showing an angry gesture against her sister's complaint. And there is no wonder in this; for Mary had another work to do that her sister knew not of. And that is why she had no leisure to listen to her nor to answer her complaint.

4. FRIEND, LET US TAKE all these words and these gestures that were disclosed between our Lord and these two sisters and make of them an example for all active persons and all contemplative persons who have been since then in the Holy Church, or who shall be until the day of judg-

ment. By Mary is understood all contemplatives; and they should make their lives conform to hers. And by Martha the active person is signified, in the same manner and for the same reason.

CHAPTER XVIII

How all active persons complain of
contemplatives just as Martha did of
Mary, but ignorance is the cause of
this complaint

1. JUST AS MARTHA COMPLAINED then about Mary her
sister, so do active persons complain about contemplative
persons unto this very day. For wherever a man or woman
in this world, whether religious or secular without ex-
ception, feels himself stirred through grace and with spiritual counsel to surrender all his outer affairs in order to
devote himself fully to living the contemplative life with
all his knowledge and conscience, all his brothers and
sisters, their close friends, and many others besides who do
not experience these urgings nor this manner of life to
which he is devoting himself will immediately rise against
him in a spirit of great complaint. They will speak sharply
to him, saying that he is doing nothing. Then they will
tell many false tales, and many true ones too, of the fall of
men and women who gave themselves to this life in the
past. But they do not tell the good tales of those who did
not fall.

2. I ADMIT that of those who forsake the world in this way many do fall and have fallen in the past. Many who should have become God's servants and His contemplatives have become the devil's servants and his contemplatives because they would not govern themselves by true spiritual understanding; and they have become either hypocrites or heretics and have fallen into frenzies and into many other kinds of mischief in slander of the Holy Church. I will not say more about this at this time, lest it obscure our subject. In what follows, nevertheless, men may see some of the conditions and the cause of their fallings as it is necessary and if God permits. We will, therefore, speak no more of these things at this time, but go on with our subject.

CHAPTER XIX

A short defense of the author teaching
that all contemplatives should excuse
all active persons of their complaining
words and deeds

1. SOME MAY THINK that I pay too little respect to
Martha, that special saint, when I compare the words in
which she complained about her sister to the words of
worldly men. I mean no disrespect, neither to her nor to
them. God forbid that I should say anything in this work
that might be construed as condemnation of any of the
servants of God in any degree, and particularly of His
special saints. It seems to me that she should be completely
excused for her complaint when we consider the time and
the circumstances in which she made it. Her lack of knowledge was the cause of what she said. And it is no wonder,
for she did not know at that time what Mary was doing.
I believe that she had heard very little of such perfection
before that time. And also the things that she said were
spoken courteously and with few words, and therefore she
must always be excused.

2. IT SEEMS TO ME that the worldly men and women who are engaged in the active life should be completely excused as well for their words of complaint of which we spoke before, even though they speak rudely the things they say as a result of their ignorance. And why is this so? Just as Martha knew very little of what Mary her sister was doing when she complained about her to our Lord, so do people nowadays know very little or nothing at all about the aims of the young disciples who set themselves apart from the business of this world and dedicate themselves to be God's special servants in holiness and rectitude of spirit. And if they would know truly, I daresay that they would neither do nor say the things they do.

3. IT SEEMS TO ME, therefore, that they must always be excused, for they know no better way of life than the one in which they themselves are engaged. And also, when I consider the innumerable faults that I myself have committed before this time in words and deeds through lack of knowledge, it seems to me that if I would be excused by God for my ignorant faults, I must always excuse other men's ignorant words and deeds with charity and pity. Otherwise I would not be doing to others as I would have them do to me.

CHAPTER XX

How Almighty God will answer those
who find excuses not to leave their
business for the love of Him

1. It seems to me therefore that those who undertake
to be contemplatives should not only forgive active men
their complaining words, but they should also be so occupied in spirit that they should pay little attention or none
at all to what men say about them or what they do. That
was what Mary who is the example for all of us did when
Martha her sister complained to our Lord. And if we will
truly do the same, our Lord will do the same for us now
as He did for Mary then.

2. What was that? Our beloved Lord Jesus Christ,
from whom no secret thing is hidden, was asked by Martha
to act as judge and to bid Mary to rise and help her serve
Him. He perceived, however, that Mary was fervently
occupied in spirit concerning the love of His Godhead
and He therefore replied courteously as was proper for
Him to do. He answered for Mary in order that she would
not need to leave the love of Him in order to excuse
herself.

3. AND HOW DID HE ANSWER? Certainly not as a judge as Martha asked Him to do, but as an advocate defending according to the law her who loved Him. "Martha, Martha!" He said. Twice for emphasis He spoke her name, for He wanted her to hear Him and take heed of His words. "You are very busy," He said, "and are troubled about many things." Those who are active persons must necessarily be busy constantly and be occupied in doing many different things, first for their own use, and then in deeds of mercy for their fellow Christians as charity requires. He said this to Martha, for He wanted her to know that the work she was doing was good and beneficial for the health of her soul; but in order that she should not think that she was engaged in the best work of all that man may do, He said further, "But one thing is necessary."

4. AND WHAT IS THAT ONE THING? Certainly that God be loved and praised of Himself above all other things physical or spiritual that man may do. And for this, in order that Martha should not think that she could both love God and praise Him above all other things physical or spiritual and be busy at the same time with the necessities of this life; and in order to free her from doubt as to whether she might not be able to serve God perfectly in both physical and spiritual affairs—imperfectly she may but not perfectly—He added that Mary had chosen the best part and that this would never be taken away from her. The reason is that this perfect stirring of love that begins here in this life is equal with that which shall last eternally in the bliss of heaven, for they both are one.

CHAPTER XXI

The true exposition of the gospel word,
"Mary has chosen the best part."

1. WHAT DOES THIS MEAN: "Mary has chosen the best part?" Wherever the best is named, two things are first required: a good and a better, so that there can be a best which is the third in number. What then are these three good things of which Mary chose the best? There are not three kinds of lives, for the Holy Church takes cognizance only of two: the active life and the contemplative life; and these two lives are expressed in a concealed way in the story of this gospel by the two sisters, Mary and Martha, Martha representing the active person and Mary the contemplative one. Without one of these two lives, no one may have salvation; and where there are no more than two, none may choose the best.

2. ALTHOUGH THERE ARE only two kinds of lives, each of these lives is divided into three parts, each one of which is better than the other. These three parts have been described in detail at an earlier point in this book. As has been said before, the first part consists in good and honest

bodily works of mercy and of charity; and this is the first degree of active life, as has been said. The second part of these two lives consists in good spiritual meditations on a man's own wretchedness, the Passion of Christ, and the joys of heaven.

3. THE FIRST PART is good, and the second part is better; for this is the second degree of the active life, and the first of the contemplative life. In this part, contemplative life and active life are coupled together in spiritual kinship and they are made sisters by the example of Mary and Martha. An active person may rise this high toward contemplation and he may come no higher except on very rare occasions, and then only by a special grace. A contemplative person may come this low toward the active life and go no lower, except very seldom in a situation of great need.

4. THE THIRD PART of these two lives is to be found in this dark cloud of unknowing with many a secret love pressed to God of Himself. The first part is good; the second part is better; but the third is best of all. This is the "best part" of Mary. It is therefore clearly to be seen that our Lord did not say that Mary has chosen the best *life*; for there are no more lives than two, and of two none may choose the best. But of these two lives, He said, Mary has chosen the best *part*, and that this shall never be taken away from her.

5. THE FIRST PART and the second part, although they are good and holy, must necessarily end with this life; for

in the other life there is no need as there is now to make use of the works of mercy, nor to weep for our wretchedness, nor for the Passion of Christ. No one will be able to be hungry then nor be thirsty then as they are now; nor will they then be able to die of cold, nor be sick, nor houseless, nor in prison; nor will they then need burial, for none shall then be able to die. But the third part that Mary chose—let it be chosen by whomever is called through grace to choose it, or let me better say, whomever is chosen to it by God. Let him turn to it with all his energies, for it shall never be taken away. If it begin here, it shall last forever.

6. THEREFORE LET THE VOICE of our Lord call on our active ones, as though He were speaking now to them for us as He did then for Mary to Martha, "Martha, Martha!" —"Active ones, Active ones! Make yourselves as busy as you can in the first part and in the second part, now in the one and now in the other, and if you are strongly inclined and feel yourself disposed, in both of them physically at once. But do not interfere with contemplatives. You do not know what is troubling them. Leave them undisturbed in their rest and in their play with the third and best part of Mary."

CHAPTER XXII

Of the wonderful love that Christ had
for man in the person of all sinners who
were truly transformed and called to
the grace of contemplation

1. SWEET WAS THE LOVE between our Lord and Mary.
She had much love for Him. He had much more for her.
Whoever would know thoroughly all that took place
between Him and her, not as a gossiper would tell it but
as the story of the gospel bears witness—which can not
possibly be false—he would find that she was so completely
desirous of loving Him that nothing less than He could
comfort her, nor could anything hold her heart from Him.
This is the same Mary who, when she sought Him at the
sepulcher with weeping hope refused to be comforted by
angels. When they spoke to her so sweetly with such great
love and said, "Weep not, Mary, for our Lord whom you
seek is risen, and you shall have Him and see Him live full
fair among His disciples as He promised," she would not
stop crying for them. And why? Her thought was that
whoever truly seeks the King of Angels will not be content to settle for angels.

2. AND WHAT MORE? Certainly whoever will look truly into the story of the gospel will find many points of perfect love written of her who is our example. These are in accord with the work of this writing as clearly as if they had been written for that very purpose. And certainly so they were, let whoever will make use of them. And if a man should desire to see written in the gospel the wonderful and special love that our Lord bore to her, the person who, of all habitual sinners, was truly transformed and called to the grace of contemplation, he will find that our Lord would not permit any man or woman—yes, not even her own sister—to speak a word against her without His answering for her Himself. Yes, and what more? He blamed Simon Leprous in his own house for what he thought against her. This was great love. This was surpassing love.

CHAPTER XXIII

How God will answer and care in spirit
for those who do not care for themselves because of their work in His love

1. IF WE WILL TRULY and determinedly make our love
and our life conform, as much as is possible for us, to the
love and the life of Mary, there is no doubt but that He
shall answer spiritually now in the same manner for us
each day secretly in the hearts of all those who either say
or think against us. I am not saying that there will not
always be someone who will say or think something against
us as long as we are engaged in the struggles of this life,
as they did against Mary. But I do say that if we will pay
no more attention to what they are saying and what they
are thinking, and if we no more cease our private spiritual
work because of their words and their thoughts than she
did—I say that then our Lord will answer them in spirit,
and if all is well with those who are speaking and thinking
this way, they will in a few days be ashamed of their words
and of their thoughts.

2. JUST AS HE WILL ANSWER for us in spirit so will He

also stir other men in spirit to give us the things that are necessary for us in this life, meat and clothes and other such things, if He sees that we will not leave the work of His love for such affairs. I say this to refute the error of those who claim that it is not lawful for men to undertake to serve God in the contemplative life unless they first secure for themselves their own bodily necessities. For they say that God sends the cow but not by the horn.* And in this they indeed speak wrongly of God, as they well know.

3. TRUST STEADFASTLY, you, whoever you may be who sincerely turns from the world to God, that God will send you either one of these two without troubling you about it: that is, either an abundance of necessities, or sufficient strength of body and patience of spirit to bear your need. What does it matter, then, which of these one has? The net result is the same in all true contemplatives. Whoever is in doubt of this either has the devil in his breast depriving him of belief, or else he is not as fully dedicated to God as he should be, no matter how clever he may be, no matter how many holy reasons he may show to the contrary, and no matter who he may be.

4. YOU, THEREFORE, having undertaken to become a contemplative as Mary was, should choose rather to be humbled under the wonderful height and worthiness of God who is perfect than under your own wretchedness which is imperfect. That is to say, take care that your particular attention is directed more to the worthiness of

---

* That is, God helps those who help themselves. A version of a medieval proverb.

God than to your own sinfulness. To those who have been made perfectly humble, nothing shall be lacking, not a physical thing and not a spiritual thing. And why? Because they have God in whom all plenty is; and whoever has Him—yes, as this book says—needs nothing else in this life.

CHAPTER XXIV

What charity is in itself, and how it is truly and perfectly contained in the work of this book

1. As it is said of humility that it is perfectly comprehended in this little blind love directed toward God when it is beating upon the dark cloud of unknowing after all other things have been put down and forgotten—so also are all other virtues to be understood, and particularly charity.

2. Charity is to signify nothing else to your understanding but love of God for Himself above all creatures, and love of man for God even as yourself. It seems very good that in this work God should be loved for Himself above all other creatures. As has been said before, the substance of this work is nothing else than a naked intent directed to God for Himself.

3. A naked intent I call it. The reason is that in this work the perfect apprentice does not seek to be released from pain nor to receive greater rewards, but he seeks

simply nothing but God Himself. In fact, he is not concerned and he does not even take notice of whether he is in pain or in bliss or whether his will has been fulfilled in what he loves. Thus it seems that in this work God is perfectly loved for Himself beyond all other creatures. For in this work, the perfect worker may not permit the memory of the holiest creature that God ever made to commune with him.

4. IT SEEMS SUFFICIENTLY INDICATED that the second and lower part of charity with respect to your fellow Christians is truly and perfectly fulfilled in this work. In this work the perfect worker shows no special favor toward any man of himself, whether he be kin or stranger, friend or foe; for he considers all men to be equally related to him, and no man to be a stranger. He considers all men to be his friends, and none to be his foes. In fact, he believes that all those who bring him pain and do him harm in this life are his full and special friends; and he is therefore inclined to will them as much good as to the closest friend he has.

CHAPTER XXV

That a perfect soul gives no special
attention to any man in this life while
engaged in this work

1. I say not that the worker in this work shall have a
special regard for any man in this life whether he be
friend or foe, kin or stranger. That cannot be if this work
is to be perfectly done, as it is when all things under God
are completely forgotten in accordance with the requirements of this work. But I do say that he shall be made so
virtuous and so charitable by the quality of this work that
his will will be strengthened accordingly. When he does
commune with or pray for his fellow Christian, he will not
do so from the midst of the work, for he may not do that
without great sin. But he will do so from the height of
this work as it is sometimes necessary to do when charity
requires it. He will do the same for his foe as for his friend,
the same to the stranger as to his kin. Indeed, he will sometimes do more for his foe than for his friend.

2. In this work, however, he is not free to distinguish
who is his friend and who is his foe, who is his kin or a

stranger. I do not say that he shall not feel at some time—in fact, quite often—a more intimate affection for one, two, or three persons; for that is lawful, and in many cases charity requires it. Christ felt such an intimate affection for John and for Mary and for Peter beyond many others. But I do say that in the actual time of doing this work all shall be equally close to him; for he shall then feel no principle but God. He shall love all clearly and purely for God, equally as much as he loves himself.

3. JUST AS ALL MANKIND was lost in Adam and as all who demonstrate by their works their desire for salvation are saved or shall be saved by virtue of the Passion of the only Christ; so also, not quite in the same manner but as though it were in the same manner, a soul that is perfectly disposed to this work and is united in this way to God in spirit as the evidence of this work testifies, does whatever it can to make all men as perfect in this work as it is itself. Just as if a limb of our body feels sore all the other limbs feel pained and diseased as well, or if a limb feels well all the others feel better too—so is it spiritually also of all the limbs of the Holy Church.

4. CHRIST IS OUR HEAD and we are the limbs if we are in charity; and whoever wishes to be a perfect disciple of our Lord will necessarily strain his spirit in this work for the salvation of all his brethren and sisters in nature, as our Lord did His body on the Cross. And in what way? Not only for His friends and his kin and his beloved ones, but generally for all mankind without any special favoritism for one more than another. All who leave sin and

seek mercy shall be saved through the virtue of His Passion.

5. WHAT IS SAID of humility and charity is to be understood also of all other virtues. All of them are truly comprehended in this small pressing of love of which we have spoken before.

CHAPTER XXVI

That without much special grace or the
continued use of common grace the
work of this book is exceedingly difficult, for it is the work of the soul
helped by grace and the work only
of God

1. WORK VERY HARD NOW for the present and beat upon
this high cloud of unknowing; then rest afterward. A
difficult task indeed does he have who commits himself to
this work. In fact, it will be exceedingly difficult unless he
either has a very special grace or he has been accustomed
to the work for a long period of time.

2. Now I ASK YOU: in what does this difficult task consist? Certainly not in that devout stirring of love that is
continually wrought in his will not by himself but by the
hand of Almighty God; for God is always ready to bring
this work to pass in each soul that is disposed to carry it
out when the person does whatever is his power and has
done so for a long time in order to carry on the work.

3. BUT I ASK YOU: in what does this difficult task consist? Certainly it consists in treading down the remembrance of all the creatures that God has ever made and in holding them beneath *the cloud of forgetting* of which we have spoken before. All the difficult work is contained in this, for this is man's fundamental struggle, with the help of grace. And the other mentioned above—that is to say, the stirring of love—that is the work only of God. Go on with your work, therefore, and surely I promise you that He shall not fail in His.

4. MOVE STEADFASTLY ahead then. Let us see how well you can carry yourself. Do you not see how He supports and sustains you? For shame! Labor hard for a while, and soon you will find that the difficulty and the pressure of this strenuous work will begin to be eased. Even though it is hard and undiminished in the beginning when you have no devotion, after a while when you have acquired devotion, what had been so hard for you will become much easier and much less taxing for you to do. You will then have little work, or perhaps none at all to do; for God will then work sometimes all by Himself. But that will not always be, nor will it be for a long period at a time. It will only be when and as He is so inclined. And then you will think it is wonderful to leave Him alone.

5. THEN WILL HE perhaps sometimes send out a beam of spiritual light piercing *the cloud of unknowing* that is between you and Him, and He will show you some of His secret ways of which man neither can nor may speak. Then

will you feel your desires inflamed with the fire of His love, far more than I can tell you, or than I can or will say at this time. For of that work which falls only to God I dare not take it upon myself to speak with my blabbering fleshly tongue. And even if I dared, I would not do so. But of that work that falls to man when he feels himself stirred and helped by grace, listen well while I tell you. For of the two, this holds less peril.

CHAPTER XXVII

Who should work in the gracious work
of this book

1. FIRST AND FOREMOST I will tell you who should take
part in this work, and when, and by what means, and
what discretion you shall have in it. If you ask me who
shall work in this, I answer: all who have forsaken the
world with a true will and who give themselves not to the
active life but to what is called the contemplative life. All
those should work in this grace and in this work, whatever
they be, and whether they be habitual sinners or not.

CHAPTER XXVIII

That a man should not presume to work
in this work before he has been lawfully
cleansed in his consciousness of all his
special deeds of sin

1. IF YOU ASK ME when one should begin this work, I answer: not before he has cleansed his consciousness, in accordance with the common ordinance of the Holy Church, of all the special deeds of sin previously committed.

2. IN THIS WORK a soul dries up within itself the entire root and ground of sin that always remains in it after confession. Therefore let whoever wishes to undertake this work first cleanse his consciousness. Afterward, when he has fulfilled what is lawfully required of him, let him give himself to the work boldly but meekly. Let him consider then that he has been held back from the work for a very long time; for this is the work in which a person should labor all his lifetime, even if he has never committed a mortal sin.

3. As long as a soul dwells in this mortal flesh, he shall see and feel this cumbrous *cloud of unknowing* between him and God. And not only that, but as a result of the original sin he shall always see and feel that some of all the creatures that God has made or some of their works are constantly pressing into his memory between him and God.

4. This is the judgment of God. When man held the sovereign power over all other creatures, he willfully submitted himself to their requests and ignored the commands of God and his Maker. Because man did this, he finds now that whenever he seeks to fulfill the bidding of God, he sees and feels all the creatures that should be beneath him proudly pressing themselves above him between him and his God.

CHAPTER XXIX

That a man should continue patiently in
this work, enduring its pain and judging
no man

1. WHOEVER DESIRES, therefore, to reach the purity
that has been lost by sin and to achieve that state of well-
being in which there is no pain must necessarily labor in
this work with great patience, enduring the pains of it no
matter how great they be, whether he has been a habitual
sinner or not.

2. EVERYONE FINDS IT DIFFICULT to do this work,
both sinners and innocent people who have hardly sinned
at all. But those who have been sinners have much greater
difficulty, and for good reason. It often happens, however,
that some who have been serious and habitual sinners reach
perfection in this work sooner than those who have not
been sinners. This is the merciful miracle of our Lord who
bestows His grace in ways that arouse the wonderment
of the world.

3. NOW TRULY I BELIEVE that the Day of Judgment

shall be fair and clear so that God will be clearly discernible with all his attributes. On that day, some who are now despised or who are valued at little or nothing as common sinners, and perhaps some who now are serious sinners shall sit side by side with saints in His sight. And, at the same itme, some of those who are now regarded among the holy, being worshiped by men as though they were angels, and some of those who perhaps have not yet committed a mortal sin shall sit mournfully among the caves of hell.

4. BY THIS YOU CAN SEE that no man should judge another here in this life, neither for the good nor the evil that he does. Only deeds may properly be judged but not the man, whether good or evil.

CHAPTER XXX

Who should criticize and condemn other men's faults

1. I ASK YOU: by whom shall men's deeds be judged? Surely by those who have the capacity and have achieved the cure of their own souls, either openly in terms of the statute and ordinance of the Holy Church, or else secretly in the spirit by the special stirring of the Holy Spirit in perfect charity.

2. LET EVERYONE BEWARE lest he presume to take it upon himself to criticize and condemn other men's faults without his having been truly touched within by the Holy Spirit in his work. Otherwise he may very easily err in his judgments. Beware therefore. Judge yourself as seems right to you between yourself and your God, and let other men alone.

CHAPTER XXXI

How a man should maintain himself
against all thoughts and stirrings of sin
when he begins this work

1. AFTER YOU HAVE REACHED THE POINT where you feel that you have done what is required of you according to the judgment of the Holy Church, you shall begin intently to carry out this work. Then if you find that particular acts that you have done in the past constantly come into your memory and come between you and your God, or that any new thought or stirring of sin does so, then you must steadfastly step above them with a fervent stirring of love and tread them down beneath your feet.

2. TRY TO COVER OVER these thoughts with a thick *cloud of forgetting* as though they had never existed neither for you nor for any other man. And if they continue to arise, continue to put them down. As often as they come up, so often must you put them down. And if you think that the labor is great, then you may seek to develop special ways, tricks, private techniques, and

spiritual devices by means of which you can put them away. And it is best to learn these methods from God by your own experience rather than from any man in this life.

CHAPTER XXXII

Concerning two spiritual devices that
are helpful for a spiritual beginner in
the work of this book

1. ALTHOUGH THIS IS SO, I will tell you what seems to me to be the best of these special ways. Test them and improve upon them if you can.

2. TRY AS MUCH AS YOU CAN to behave as though you are not aware that these thoughts are pressing so strongly upon you between you and your God. Try to look, as it were, over their shoulders, as though you were looking for somethings else; and this other thing is God enclosed in a *cloud of unknowing*. If you do this, I believe that in a short time your labor will be greatly eased. I believe that when this method is correctly understood and practiced it involves nothing else than a longing desire for God, to feel Him and to see Him as much as is possible in this life. Such a desire is charity, and it always merits fulfillment.

3. THERE IS ANOTHER METHOD, and you may test it if you wish. When you feel that you are altogether unable to press down your thoughts, cower beneath them cringing

as a coward overcome in battle. Think then that it is foolishness for you to strive any longer with them, and yield yourself therefore to God in the hands of your enemies. Regard yourself then as one who has been lost forever.

4. TAKE THE GREATEST CARE in using this method, however, for it seems to me that in applying it you can melt all things to water. But when this method is correctly conceived it becomes nothing else than a true knowledge and feeling of yourself as you are, a wretch and a filthy thing far worse than nothing. This knowledge and feeling is meekness. And this meekness results in God Himself coming down with great strength to avenge you on your enemies, to raise you up and with loving care dry your spiritual eyes, as the father does to his child about to perish at the mouths of wild beasts.

CHAPTER XXXIII

That in this work a person is cleansed
both of his special sins and of their
pain, and that there is no perfect rest
in this life

1. I WILL NOT TELL YOU of any more methods at this time. If you possess the grace with which to practice these, I am sure that you will be better able to teach me than I am to teach you. Even though it should not be so, yet it seems to me truly that I am very far from the goal. I therefore beg of you to help me and to labor for yourself as well as for me.

2. CARRY ON THEN, do the hard labor now, and suffer meekly the pain that is necessary if you are to succeed with these methods. Truly, this is your purgatory. When the painful time has passed and your practices are as though they were given to you by God and graciously come to you out of habit, I have no doubt but that you will be cleansed not only of sin but of the pain of sin. I mean of the pain of your particular sins committed in the past, and not the pain of the original sin. That pain shall remain

with you to the day of your death no matter what you do. It shall be of little trouble to you, however, in comparison with the pain of your special sins; and yet you shall not be left without great and difficult labor.

3. OUT OF THE ORIGINAL SIN there will continually spring new and fresh stirrings of sin; and it will be necessary for you constantly to strike them down, cutting them down with a sharp, double-edged and dreadful sword of knowledge and will. By this you may see and learn that there is no steady security and no true rest in this life.

4. YOU SHALL NOT RETREAT because of this, however, nor shall you have great fear of failure. For if you have the grace with which to overcome in the manner described earlier the pain of the particular sins you have committed in the past—or better still, if you are able to improve upon these methods—then you may be sure that the pain of the original sin or the new stirrings of sin that are to come will have very little power to provoke you.

CHAPTER XXXIV

That God gives this grace freely with
no special methods and that it may not
be achieved by means of them

1. IF YOU ASK ME by what means you are to come to this work, I pray that Almighty God in His great grace and goodness will teach you Himself. In fact, it is best for you to know that I cannot tell you. The reason is that it is the work only of God especially wrought in the soul that He desires, and this without respect to the merit of the soul. Without this grace, no saint or angel can conceive of seeking it. And I believe that our Lord particularly and often—yes, more particularly and more often—permits this work to be carried through in those who have been habitual sinners than in those who have brought Him comparatively little grief. This He does, for He is all-merciful and almighty; and He works as He wishes, where He wishes, and when He wishes.

2. HE DOES NOT GIVE THIS GRACE, however, nor take part in this work with any person who is unable to do it. And yet there is no soul without this grace, for all are

capable of it whether a sinner's soul or an innocent's soul. It is not given as a reward for innocence, nor is it withheld because of sin.

3. NOTE CAREFULLY that I say withheld and withdrawn. Take care to beware of error here. It is always so that the nearer men come to truth, the more it is necessary for them to beware of error. I mean well for you. If you cannot conceive it, lay it aside until God comes and teaches it to you. Do that and do not harm yourself.

4. BEWARE OF PRIDE, for it blasphemes the gifts of God and makes sinners bold. If you are truly meek, your feelings about this work will agree with my statement that God gives it freely without its being merited. The nature of this work is such that its presence enables a soul both to have it and to feel it. And no soul may have that capacity without it. The ability to do this work is inherently contained in the work itself so that whoever feels this work is thereby enabled to do it, and no one else. In fact, without this work a soul is dead, as it were, and can neither covet it nor desire it.

5. TO THE DEGREE that you will it and desire it, you have that much of it; no more and no less. And yet it is not a matter of will, nor a matter of desire, but something, you never know what, that stirs you to desire and to will a thing you never know. Pay no heed to this, I beg of you, if you know no more; but go onward, do more and more, and keep yourself active.

6. THE BRIEFEST WAY for me to put it is this: let that thing do with you whatever it wishes and let it lead you wherever it wishes. Let *it* be the active one, and you be but the passive one. Do nothing more than observe it and let it alone. Do not interfere with it thinking you will help it. Beware of doing that, lest you spoil everything.

7. YOU BE BUT THE TREE and let it be the caretaker. You be but the house, and let it be the squire dwelling within. Be blind at this time and cut away all desire for knowledge, for that will hinder you much more than it will help you. It is quite sufficient that you feel yourself so strongly stirred by a thing of whose nature you know nothing at all. In this way, the stirring within you carries no special thought of anything under God, and thus your intent is directed purely toward God.

8. IF THIS IS THE CASE, trust steadfastly that it is clearly only God who is stirring your will and your desire of Himself with no special devices being used, neither by Him nor by you. And have no fear, for the devil is not able to come so near. He comes to stir a man's will only very seldom, and then from afar, no matter how clever a devil he may be. Without special devices, neither can a good angel stir your will strongly enough; in fact, nothing can do so, but only God.

9. FROM THESE WORDS it is now possible for you to conceive in general (and you will understand it much more clearly from your practice) that in this work men are not

to use any special devices, for subtle methods will not lead them to it. All good procedures derive from it, but it itself depends on none; and there are no special methods that lead to it.

CHAPTER XXXV

Concerning the three practices with
which a contemplative disciple should
be occupied: reading, thinking, and
praying

1. THERE ARE METHODS, however, which a student in contemplation may practice, and these are: Lesson, Meditation, and Orison; or you may call them: Reading, Thinking, and Praying. You shall find these three things described much better than I can in another book by another man. It is, therefore, not necessary for me here to tell you the details of them.

2. THIS MUCH I WILL TELL YOU, however. These three are bound together in such a way that, for those who are beginners and for those who are advancing in the work—but not for those who are perfect in the sense that we have described it here—the stage of thinking can be reached only after reading and hearing. Reading and hearing are essentially the same: the clergyman reads in books, while illiterate men read by means of the clergyman when they hear him preach the word of God. But

143

prayer may not be achieved, neither in beginners nor in advanced students, unless thinking comes first. Verify this with your experience.

3. IN THIS CONTEXT, God's word whether written or spoken may be compared to a mirror. Spiritually, the eyes of your soul are your reason, your consciousness is your spiritual face. And just as it is so that if you have a dirty spot on your physical face your eyes cannot see that spot nor know where it is without a mirror or someone else to tell you; so it is spiritually in the same way that without reading or hearing God's word it is not possible for a soul blinded by habitual sin to see the foul spot upon his consciousness.

4. IN ACCORDANCE WITH THIS, when a man looks into a physical or a spiritual mirror or learns from what other men tell him where the foul spot is on his face, physically or spiritually, he runs at once to the well to wash himself, but not before he knows where the spot is. If this spot involves a special sin, then the well is the Holy Church and the water is the confession with all its attendant circumstances. But if this spot is only a blind root and a stirring of sin, then the well is the merciful God and the water is prayer with all its circumstances. You can see from this that good thinking cannot be achieved, neither by beginner nor by advanced students, without their first reading and hearing. And, in the same way, praying cannot come before thinking.

CHAPTER XXXVI

Concerning the meditations of those who are continually engaged in the work of this book

1. THIS IS NOT THE CASE, however, with those who continually carry out the work of this book. Their meditations come as though they were spontaneous thoughts and unguided feelings concerning their own wretchedness or the goodness of God. They come neither from reading nor from listening, nor are they beholden to any special thing under God.

2. THESE SPONTANEOUS THOUGHTS and unguided feelings come to one much more from God than from man. It is not necessary for you ever to have meditated on your wretchedness nor on the goodness of God, assuming that you are a person who is stirred by grace and works with spiritual guidance. It is necessary only that you meditate on the word SIN or on the word GOD, or on any comparable words that you may prefer, not analyzing or interpreting them with refinements of learning, but simply considering the qualities of the words with the earnest intention of increasing your devotion.

3. I BELIEVE that one should never analyze intellectually in this work. Rather, consider these words as wholes. Think of sin as a *lump*, a thing you know not what, that is, nonetheless, nothing else but yourself. While you are engaged in this blind beholding of sin considered as an entity, a *lump* that is nothing else than yourself, you will no doubt appear to be as distracted as any mad person who ever was bound. But it is also possible that if you do this work without changing your countenance, those who see you will think of you as being completely sober and relaxed, whether you are sitting or walking, lying or leaning, standing or kneeling in the work.

CHAPTER XXXVII

Concerning the special prayers of those
who are continually engaged in the
work of this book

1. JUST AS THE MEDITATIONS OF THOSE who continually labor in this grace and in this work appear
suddenly without any preparation, their prayers come in
the same way. I mean their own, personal prayers, not the
prayers that are ordained by the Holy Church. Those who
truly practice this work do not worship by prayer very
much. They pray according to the form and the law that
has been ordained by the holy fathers before us; but their
special prayers always rise spontaneously to God without
having been planned in advance, and without any particular
techniques either preceding them or accompanying them.

2. WHEN THESE PRAYERS ARE IN WORDS, as they
very seldom are, they are only in very few words; in fact,
the fewer the better. Indeed, if it is but a little word of
one syllable it seems to me to be better than a word of
two syllables or more. This is in accordance with the work
of the spirit, for a spiritual worker should always be at the
highest and ultimate point of the spirit.

3. You CAN SEE that this is so by an example drawn from the course of nature. When a man or a woman is overcome by fear in any sudden emergency such as fire, a person dying, or anything of that kind, he is impelled immediately to cry out from the intensity of his feeling calling for help to come at once. Yes, and how does he do this? Certainly it is not in many words; and it is not even in one word of two syllables. The reason is that it would take him too long should he try to explain the nature of his need. He therefore bursts out all at once with a great spirit and cries a little word of one syllable, such as the word "fire" or the word "help."

4. AND JUST AS THIS LITTLE WORD "fire" stirs and pierces the ears of the hearers much more quickly, so does a little word of one syllable do the same when it is not only spoken or thought but secretly intended in the depth of the spirit. This depth is height, for spiritually all is one, height and depth, length and breadth. It pierces the ears of the Almighty God more than does any psalter thoughtlessly mumbled in one's teeth. This is the reason it is written that *short prayer pierces heaven.*

CHAPTER XXXVIII

How and why short prayer pierces heaven

1. AND WHY DOES IT PIERCE HEAVEN, this little short prayer of one small syllable? Surely because it is prayed with a full spirit, in the height and in the depth, in the length and in the breadth of the spirit of him who prays it. It is in the height, for it is with all the power of the spirit. It is in the depth, for in this one little syllable all the knowledge of the spirit is contained. It is in the length, for no matter when it would feel as it does feel it would cry just as it cries. It is in the breadth, for it wills to everyone the same that it wills to itself.

2. IT IS IN THIS TIME that a soul has comprehended the lesson of Saint Paul and all the saints—not fully, but in some manner and in part in accordance with the degree of his work—concerning what is the length and the breadth, the height and the depth of the everlasting and all-loving, almighty and all-knowing God. The everlastingness of God in His length. His love is His breadth. His power is His height. And His wisdom is His depth.

3. IT IS NO WONDER that a soul that conforms so closely by grace to the image and likeness of God his maker should soon be heard by God. Even if it were a sinful soul—which is, as it were, an enemy of God—if he might by means of grace be able to cry such a little syllable in the height and the depth, the length and the breadth of his spirit, he would always be heard and helped by God because of the terrible noise of his cry.

4. LET US TAKE AN EXAMPLE. If you hear a man who is your mortal enemy cry out through fear in the height of his spirit the little word "fire" or the word "help," you will come to help him. It will not be because you are concerned about him, for he is your enemy; but it will be because of the pure pity that is stirred in your heart and raised by the dolefulness of his cry that you will get up—yes, even if it is a mid-winter's night—and help him to put out his fire or to calm and quiet him in his distress.

5. OH LORD! if a man can be made so merciful in grace as to have so much mercy and so much pity on his enemy despite his enmity, what pity and what mercy shall God have for a spiritual cry in the soul made and uttered in the height and the depth, in the length and the breadth of his spirit, considering that God has by nature all that man has only by grace? Much more certainly beyond comparison, much more mercy will He have, for the thing that is had by nature is much closer to the eternal thing than that which is had by grace.

CHAPTER XXXIX

How a perfect worker is to pray, and
what prayer is in itself; and if a man
prays in words, which words are most
fitting for prayer

1. THIS IS WHY WE SHOULD PRAY in the height and the
depth, the length and the breadth of our spirit, not in
many words but in a short word of one syllable.

2. AND WHAT SHALL THIS WORD BE? Certainly it shall
be such a word as best fits the nature of prayer. And what
word is that? Let us first see what prayer is in itself, and
then we will be able to know more clearly which word
will best accord with the nature of prayer.

3. PRAYER IN ITSELF PROPERLY is nothing else than a
devout intention directed toward God to receive good
and remove evil. Since all evil is comprehended in sin,
either by cause or by being, let us therefore say, or think,
or mean, when we wish to pray intently to remove evil,
only this little word "sin." And if we wish to pray intently
to receive good, let us cry either with word or thought,

or desire no other word and no more words but this one word, "God." This is because all good is in God, either by cause or by being.

4. Do not marvel then at my reason for setting these words beyond all others. If I could find any shorter words that would comprehend all good and all evil within them as fully as these words do, or if I had been taught by God to take any other words either, I would have taken those and discarded these. And I advise you to do the same.

5. Do not study mere words, for you will never achieve your purpose in this work that way. It is never achieved by study, but only by grace. Therefore, even though I have set forth certain words here, you must not pray with any other words but those that you are stirred by God to take. If God should stir you to take these, I do not advise you to ignore them. I mean if you wish to pray in words; otherwise not, for these are very short words.

6. Even though the brevity of prayer is greatly recommended here, we do not place any limit on the frequency of prayer. As has been said before, the prayer is to be prayed in the length of the spirit, and this means that it should never cease until it receives all that it is seeking. We have an example of this in the man or the woman who is afraid in the manner we described above. They never cease crying the little word "help" or the little word "fire" until they have received some help in their trouble.

CHAPTER XL

When a person is engaged in this work,
he is to give no special attention to any
vice in itself nor to any virtue in itself

1. YOU SHOULD UNDERSTAND the word "sin" in the
same spiritual sense as referring to sin in general and not
to a particular kind of sin, whether venial or mortal: pride,
anger, or envy, covetousness, sloth, gluttony, or lust. What
does it matter to a contemplative person which sin or how
many sins he has? He considers all sins to be equally great
in themselves—I mean during the course of this work—
since the least sin separates him from God and deprives
him of his spiritual peace.

2. FEEL SIN TO BE A LUMP, a thing you know not what
that is nothing but yourself. Then constantly call out this
one spiritual cry, "Sin, sin, sin! Out, out, out!" You will
find with experience that you can learn this spiritual cry
much better from God than from the teaching of any man.
It is best when it comes in a pure spirit without any special
thought and even without actually pronouncing a word,
except on those infrequent occasions when both body and

soul are filled with sorrow and the heaviness of sin, and then, out of the fullness of the spirit, it bursts out in a spoken word.

3. PROCEED IN THE SAME MANNER with this little word, "God." Fill yourself with the spiritual meaning of it without any special attention to any of His works, whether they be good, better, or the best of all; and whether they be physical or spiritual, and whether they be achieved in man's soul by grace. Do not look to see whether it is meekness or charity, patience or abstinence, hope, faith, or soberness, chastity, or voluntary poverty. What does this matter to contemplatives? They find and feel all virtues in God, for everything is in Him both by cause and by being. They think that if they have God they have all good and therefore they have no special desires for anything but only for Good God. Do the same yourself as far as you are able to by grace. Intend God altogether, and all God, so that nothing works in your mind, but only God.

4. IT WILL ALWAYS BE NECESSARY for you to feel this foul stinking lump of sin to some degree as long as you are living in this wretched life, for sin is permanently united with the substance of your being. Alternate in your mind, therefore, the two words: sin and God. And do so with the understanding that if you have God, you will have no sin; and if you have no sin, you will have God.

CHAPTER XLI

In all other works beneath this, men
have some leeway; but in this they
have none

1. IF YOU ASK ME FURTHER what leeway you have for
your own judgment in this work, my answer is, none at
all. You are permitted a freedom of decision in the other
things that you do, such as, in eating and drinking, in
sleeping and in protecting your body from extremes of
cold or heat, and in the length of prayer and reading and
in conversation with your fellow Christians. In all these
things you may use your own discretion to see that they
are neither too much nor too little. But in this work you
are to make no measures, for you are not to stop it at
all as long as you live.

2. I DO NOT SAY that you are always to continue in it
with equal strength, for that is not possible. There will
be times when sickness and other unavoidable conditions
of the body and soul with many other necessities of nature
will hinder you a great deal, and often they will draw you
down from the height of this work. What I do say, how-

ever, is that one way or another you should constantly be engaged in it, whether in actual working or in your will. For the love of God, therefore, be as careful as you possibly can be where sickness is concerned so that you will not be the cause of your own weakness. I tell you truthfully that this work requires a great calmness, an integrated and clean disposition, both in body and in soul.

3. FOR THE LOVE OF GOD, therefore, regulate yourself prudently both in body and in soul and secure your health as much as you can. And if beyond your power sickness does come to you, be patient and await God's mercy with meekness. At such times, everything is good enough. In fact, it is often true that patience in sickness and in other kinds of trouble is much more pleasing to God than any other devotion you might make when you have your health.

CHAPTER XLII

That by not varying in this work man
shall have freedom in all other things;
and otherwise none at all

1. PERHAPS YOU WILL NOW ASK ME how you are to
regulate yourself in food and in sleep, and in all other
things of that kind. The answer is brief: Do the best that
you can. Practice this work without stop and without
measure, and then you will know how to control all your
other works with great judgment. I think that a person who
perseveres in this work night and day without limit cannot
possibly fall into error in these outward doings. Otherwise,
it seems to me, he would always be in error.

2. IF I EVER ACHIEVED an alert and active concentration
on this spiritual work within my soul, it would then not
matter at all what I did in eating or in drinking, in sleeping
or in speaking, or in any of my outward activities. And
certainly I can tell you that I would much rather attain
freedom in these things in this way, by not needing to be
concerned about them, than by concentrating a great deal
of attention on them. In fact, if I go about it with such

deliberateness, marking and measuring my acts in these things, I would never succeed in my work no matter what I might do or say.

3. LET MEN SAY WHAT THEY WILL, but let practice be the proof. Lift up your heart, therefore, with a blind stirring of love, thinking of sin and God. You are seeking God, and hoping to be rid of sin. But it is sin that you are sure of having, and it is God you lack. Now may the good God help you, for now you are in need.

CHAPTER XLIII

That all knowing and feeling of a man's own being must be lost if the perfection of this work is to be truly felt by any man in this life

1. TAKE CARE that nothing is active in your mind or in your will but only God. Try to strike down all your knowing and feeling of everything under God, and tread everything down far beneath the cloud of forgetting. Then you will understand that in this work you are not only to forget all creatures other than yourself, their deeds and your own deeds as well; but in this work you are also to forget both yourself and your deeds for God as well as all other creatures and their deeds. For the sign of a perfect lover is not only that he loves the thing he loves more than he loves himself, but also, in a sense, that he hates himself on behalf of the thing he loves.

2. THIS IS WHAT YOU ARE TO DO with yourself. You shall loathe and be impatient with everything that is active in your mind and in your will unless it is God. Anything else, whatever it may be, will come between you and your

God. It is no wonder, then, that you should loathe and hate to think of yourself, for you always feel sin as a foul stinking lump of you know not what, intruding between you and your God. And this lump is nothing else than yourself. For you must realize that sin is permanently united with the substance of your being so that it will never leave you.

3. DESTROY THEREFORE all your knowing and feeling of every kind of creature, and especially of yourself. Your thinking and feeling of all other creatures depends on your awareness of yourself, for when you have overcome that, all other creatures can easily be forgotten. If you will actively apply yourself to practice this, you will find that when you have forgotten all other creatures and all their words—and as a matter of fact, all your own works as well—there will still remain between you and your God a pure awareness and feeling of your own being. And this awareness and feeling must necessarily be overcome before you can experience the work steadfastly in its perfection.

CHAPTER XLIV

How a soul is to destroy all knowing and feeling of its own being

1. Now you ask me how you can destroy this pure awareness and feeling of your own being. Perhaps you think that if it were destroyed all other hindrances would also be destroyed; and if you think that, you are correct. But in this regard I must tell you that without a very special grace given by God without restriction, and also without an adequate capacity on your part making you capable of receiving this grace, this pure awareness and feeling of your being cannot possibly be destroyed.

2. This ability is not less than a strong and profound spiritual sorrow. You must use your discretion, however, where this sorrow is concerned. Take care, when this sorrow comes upon you, that you do not strain your body or your spirit too violently. Instead you should sit completely still as though you had fallen asleep, worn out by crying, and sunken in your sorrow. This is true sorrow; this is perfect sorrow. To achieve this sorrow is a very great thing.

3. ALL MEN HAVE REASON FOR SORROW, but most particularly does he have cause for sorrow who knows and feels that he *is*. Compared to this, all other sorrows are mere sport. When he knows and feels not only what he is but that he is, a man can experience sorrow authentically. And whoever has never felt this sorrow, truly has reason to be sad; for he has not yet felt the ultimate sorrow. This sorrow, when it is experienced, cleanses the soul not only of sin but also of the pain that derives from sin. And it thereby makes a soul capable of receiving that joy that separates a man from the awareness and feeling of his being.

4. WHEN THIS SORROW is truly conceived it is full of holy desire; otherwise a man in this life might not be able to bear it. If it were not that the soul receives a certain amount of comfort from properly doing the work, he would not be able to bear the pain that comes from being aware of and feeling his being. The reason for this is that, whenever he seeks to have a true knowledge and feeling of his God in purity of spirit, as much as may be in this life, he realizes that he cannot have it. He discovers time and again that his awareness and his feeling are occupied and filled with a foul stinking lump of himself that must be hated and despised and forsaken if he is to be God's perfect disciple knowing God Himself upon the mount of perfection.

5. AND WHENEVER HE REALIZES THIS, he goes practically mad for sorrow. He weeps then, and he wails; he struggles and curses profanely. It seems to him, in fact,

that he is bearing so heavy a burden of himself that he does not care at all what happens to him; and then it is that God is pleased. And yet, in all this sorrow, he does not desire to cease to exist; for that would be the devil's madness and spitefulness toward God. He wishes very much to be, and he offers his thanks to God with all his heart for the great worth and the gift of his being. But he does desire unceasingly to be rid of the awareness and the feeling of his being.

6. EVERY SOUL NEEDS TO HAVE and to feel within itself this sorrow and this desire, either in the above manner or in some other. God undertakes to teach his spiritual disciples according to His good will and according to the degree and nature of their abilities in body and soul. This is with the purpose that eventually they may be united with God in perfect charity, as much as may be in this life, if God makes it possible.

CHAPTER XLV

A good statement of some deceptions
that occur in this work

1. ONE THING I will tell you. A young disciple who
has not practiced this spiritual work long enough to become experienced in it may very easily be deceived. If he
does not proceed with great caution, and if he does not
have the grace to discontinue the work and humbly seek
advice, his bodily powers may quite possibly be destroyed
while his spiritual faculties fall into fantasy. All this has to
do with pride, sensuality, and intellectual curiosity.

2. THIS IS THE WAY the deception may come to pass.
A young man or a woman who has newly undertaken the
study of devotion hears this sorrow and desire read and
spoken of, telling how a man shall lift up his heart to God
and unceasingly desire to feel the love of his God. Caught
then in the grip of an intellectual curiosity, they understand
these words not spiritually as they were intended, but
sensually and physically. Their physical hearts are then
greatly excited in their breasts. And then, because of a
lack of grace, and because of their pride and curiosity,

they strain their veins and their bodily powers in such improper and inordinate ways that they fall either into frenzies, weariness, or a kind of debility in which they lose all desires of body or soul.

3. THIS MAKES THEM GO OUT of themselves and seek some false and vain physical pleasure on the outside, as it were, for the recreation of their body and spirit. Otherwise, if they do not fall into this, then, as a result of their spiritual blindness and the sensual chafing of their physical natures from doing this false and vulgar nonspiritual work, their breasts are inflamed by an unnatural heat caused by their misuse of their bodies in this pretended work, or else there comes into them a false heat created by the devil, their spiritual enemy, and brought about by their pride, their sensuality, and their curiosity of mind.

4. SOMETIMES THEY THINK that this is the fire of love received and kindled by the grace and goodness of the Holy Spirit. Truly, from this deception and from its branches, many mischiefs come, much hypocrisy, much heresy, and much error. For just as a true knowledge follows a true feeling in the school of God, so does a false knowledge come immediately after a false feeling in the school of the devil. I tell you truly that the devil has his contemplatives just as God has His.

5. THE DECEPTION OF FALSE FEELING and of false knowledge that follows upon it has many amazing variations, depending on the diverse conditions of those who are deceived, just as there is a great variety in the true

feelings and knowledge of those who achieve salvation. I do not wish to discuss here, however, any deceptions other than those which I believe will assail you in the course of this work if you actually undertake it. Of what value would it be for you to know how these great scholars and men and women of other degrees than yours are deceived? Surely it is of no value at all, and that is why I will tell you only of those that may pertain to you when you are engaged in the work. I mention this to you now so that you will know to be very cautious about these things in your work if they should assail you.

CHAPTER XLVI

A good teaching concerning how a man
can avoid these deceptions and work
with a spiritual desire rather than with a
boisterousness of body

1. FOR THE LOVE OF GOD, therefore, be careful in this
work and do not strain your fleshly heart in a tempestuous
way without moderation. Work more with a desire than
with futile strength. The greater your desire, the more
humbly and spiritually you will work; and the more ig-
norantly you proceed, the more physical and vulgar will
be your work.

2. BE CAREFUL, therefore. Any vulgar heart that pre-
sumes to touch the high mount of this work will surely
be beaten away with stones. Stones are hard by nature,
and they hurt very much where they hit. Certainly such
vulgar strainings are closely bound to the feelings of the
flesh and are devoid of a knowledge of grace. They hurt
the foolish soul and make it fester in fantasies constructed
by the devil.

3. BE CAREFUL, therefore, with these vulgar ways, and learn to love with a mild and gentle desire expressed both in your body and in your soul. Await the will of our Lord meekly and attentively, and do not snatch overhastily as though you were a greedy greyhound, no matter how hungry you may be. Stating it lightly, I advise that you express what is in yourself, and avoid any vulgar or violent stirring of your spirit, just as you would certainly not let Him know now how very much you wish to see Him and have Him and feel Him.

4. YOU MAY THINK, perhaps, that this is childishly and playfully spoken. I believe, however, that whoever will have the grace to do and feel as I say will make most pleasant play with Him, kissing and embracing as the father does with the child.

CHAPTER XLVII

A slight teaching of this work in purity
of spirit, explaining how a person is to
show his desire to God, and on the other
hand, to man

1. CONSIDER NOW why I speak so childishly, as though
I were foolish and without common sense. I do it for
certain reasons, for it seems to me that I have been stirred
for many days to feel and think this way and to say this
to some of my other special friends in God as well as to
you.

2. ONE REASON for which I tell you to hide from God
the desire of your heart is the following. I have the hope
that by hiding it, the knowledge of it will reach Him more
clearly for your advantage in fulfilling your desire than
it would by your displaying it, at least, I believe, by any
of the means of displaying it of which you are capable at
this time. Another reason is that, by having you show it
in a hidden way I would hope to lead you away from the
boisterousness of physical feeling and toward the purity
and depth of spiritual feeling. And thus I would hope

ultimately to help you tie the spiritual knot of burning love between you and your God in spiritual unity and harmony of will.

3. You know well that God is a Spirit, and that anyone who desires to be united with Him must necessarily keep himself steadfastly in depth of spirit and far from all counterfeit physical things. Surely everything is known to God, and nothing, neither physical nor spiritual things, may be hidden from His knowledge. And since God is a Spirit, the thing that is hidden in the depth of the spirit is more openly known and shown to Him than things that are in contact with the physical in any degree. By their very nature, therefore, physical things are further from God than are spiritual things. It seems, consequently, that when our desires have physical qualities mingled with them, as they do when we stress and strain ourselves in spirit and body together, we are then further from God than we would be if we proceeded more devoutly and soberly in purity and depth of spirit.

4. You can now perceive at least partially why I instructed you so childishly to conceal from God the stirring of your desire. And yet I have not told you to hide it completely, for it would be the instructions of a fool to tell you to do what cannot be done. I have told you, rather, to do whatever you are able to do to hide it. And why have I said that? Certainly because I want you to press it deep into your spirit far from contamination with physical things, which would make it less spiritual and take it that much further from God; and also because

I know well that the greater the spiritual quality of your soul, the less is its physical quality. The nearer then it is to God, the more pleasing it is to Him, and the more clearly it can be seen by Him. Not that His sight may be clearer at one time than at another, nor clearer in one thing than in another thing, for it never changes. It is merely that your soul accords with Him better when it is in purity of Spirit, for He is a Spirit.

5. THERE IS ANOTHER REASON for which I tell you to do whatever you can not to let Him know. You and I and a great many others among us have so great a tendency to understand a thing in physical terms when it has been spoken spiritually that perhaps if I had told you to show God the stirring of your heart you would have shown it to Him physically, either by a gesture, or your voice, or in a word, or in some other vulgar bodily expression, as you would do if you wished to disclose something hidden in your heart to a physical person. And if you had done that, you would be impure. Things are to be shown in one way to man and in another way to God.

CHAPTER XLVIII

How God will be served both with
body and with soul, and will reward
men with both; and how men shall
know whether the sounds and sweetness
that come into the body in the course
of prayer are good or evil

1. I DO NOT SAY THIS because I want you to desist if at
any time you feel stirred to pray with your mouth, or to
burst out in the full devotion of your spirit and speak to
God as to a man and say some good word that may come
to you, such words as, "Good Jesus! Fair Jesus! Sweet
Jesus!" and the like. No, may God forbid that you take
it that way, for truly I do not mean that, and may God
forbid that I should separate the body and the spirit which
God has joined together.

2. GOD WISHES TO BE SERVED with both the body and
the spirit together, as is proper, and He will give man his
reward in bliss both in body and in soul. In giving that
reward, He sometimes inflames the body of His devout
servants with wonderful pleasures here in this life, not only

once or twice, but very often in some cases as He may wish. Of these pleasures not all come into the body from outside through the windows of our senses, but come from within, rising and springing up out of an abundance of spiritual gladness and out of true devotion in the spirit. Such pleasures are not to be held suspect. In fact, I am sure that whoever has such pleasures will not be suspicious of them.

3. ALL OTHER PLEASURES, however, all sounds and gaiety and sweetness that come from the outside suddenly without your knowing from whence they come, of all these I ask you to be suspicious. They may be either good or evil. If they have been made by a good angel, they will be good; if they have been made by an evil angel, they will be evil. But they will not be evil at all if the deceptions that come from curiosity of mind or from inordinate straining of the fleshly heart are removed in the manner that I have instructed you, or in some better manner if you are able to devise one.

4. WHY IS THIS SO? The reason lies in the cause of this pleasure, that is, the devout stirring of love that arises in the pure spirit. It is made by the hand of almighty God with no special methods, and it is necessary, therefore, to keep yourself far from any fantasy or any false opinion that may come to man in this life.

5. WITH REGARD to the other pleasures of various kinds and how you are to tell which are good and which are evil, I will not speak of them at this time. It does not seem

to me to be necessary, for you will find them described in another book written by another man a thousand times better than I can say or write, just as you may be able to write what I have set forth here much better than I have done. But what does that matter? I shall not stop my writing because of that, nor shall it disturb me in fulfilling the desire and stirring of your heart, which you have already shown yourself to have toward me, first with your words and now with your deeds.

6. THIS MAY I SAY TO YOU, however, with regard to those sounds and sweetnesses that come into you through the windows of your senses, and which may be either good or evil. Constantly be engaged with this blind and devout and desirous stirring of love of which I tell you, and in time we will be able to talk about these things. And if, nonetheless, you are astonished by them in the early stages —for they are quite out of the ordinary—that will be a benefit for you. It will serve to hold your heart firmly within bounds so that you will thereafter place no stock in such things without first verifying them either within yourself wonderfully through the spirit of God or else with the guidance of some discreet father.

CHAPTER XLIX

The substance of all perfection is
nothing else than a good will, and all
the comforts that occur in the course
of life are as though they were nothing
more than accidents

1. I IMPLORE, therefore, that you give yourself with a full desire to this meek stirring of love which is in your heart, and follow it. It will be your guide in this life and it will bring you happiness in the next. It is the substance of all good living, and without it no good work can be begun or ended. It is nothing else than a good will in accord with God with a feeling in your will of being well content with everything He does.

2. SUCH A GOOD WILL is the substance of all perfection. Compared to this, all sweetness and pleasures physical or spiritual are little more than incidental, no matter how holy they may be. They all depend on this good will. I say they are only incidental because they may be had or not had without causing any harm. I mean in this life, for this is not the case in the bliss of heaven; there they are united

with the substance and are never separated from it as the body in which they now work is eventually separated from the soul.

3. IN THIS LIFE, therefore, their substance is only a good spiritual will. I strongly believe that whoever experiences the perfection of this will to the degree to which that is possible in this life, will regard all human pleasures impartially, feeling equally happy either to have or not to have them according to God's will.

CHAPTER L

What chaste love is, and how in some
creatures sensual comforts come but seldom whereas in others they come often

1. YOU CAN SEE FROM THIS that we ought to direct all
our attention to this meek stirring of love in our will.
Toward all other sweetness and pleasures, physical or
spiritual, no matter how pleasing nor how holy they may
be, we should have an attitude of unconcern. If they come,
welcome them; but do not depend on them lest it weaken
you, for it will take up a great deal of your strength if
you remain with these sweet pleasures for a long time.

2. IT MAY BE ALSO that you will be stirred to love God
for their sake, and if that is the case, you will be able to
recognize it by the fact that you will complain too much
when they are gone. That will indicate that your love has
not yet become either pure or perfect. For a love that is
pure and perfect may permit its body to be fed and comforted by sweet feelings and pleasures; but it will not
complain, for it will be equally pleased to be without
these pleasures at God's will. Nonetheless, this love often

comes with such pleasures in some persons while in other persons these pleasures are very seldom had.

3. ALL THIS IS IN ACCORD with the principles and will of God to meet the needs of diverse kinds of people. Some persons are so weak and tender of spirit that if they were not comforted by some feelings of pleasure they would not be able to bear the diversity of temptations and troubles that they encounter at the hands of their physical and spiritual enemies in this life, and that they must endure. There are some who are so weak in their body that they are not able to perform any great penance by which to cleanse themselves; and our Lord cleanses these people very graciously in spirit by means of sweet feelings and tears. On the other hand, there are some persons who are so strong in spirit that they can derive sufficient pleasure for themselves within their own souls by offering this reverent and meek stirring of love and their will in accord with God. They do not need to be sustained by pleasures in their bodily feelings. Which of these is holier and more precious to God, God knows and I do not.

CHAPTER LI

That men should take great care not to
interpret in a physical way a thing that
is meant spiritually, and particularly to
be careful in understanding the word
"in" and the word "up"

1. DIRECT YOURSELF HUMBLY, therefore, to this blind
stirring of love in your heart. I mean not in your physical
heart but in your spiritual heart, which is your will. And
be especially careful lest you interpret in a physical sense
things that have been spoken spiritually. Truly I tell you
that the physical and sensual conceptions of those who
have curious and imaginative minds can be the cause of
considerable error.

2. YOU CAN SEE AN EXAMPLE of this in my instructing
you to hide your desire from God within yourself. Perhaps, if I had instructed you to show your desire to God,
you would have thought of it in a more physical way than
you do now since I have told you to hide it. You know
well that when a thing is deliberately hidden it is placed
in the depths of the spirit. That is why it seems to me to

be especially necessary that we be careful in our understanding of words that are spoken with a spiritual meaning so that we will not understand them in a physical sense but in a spiritual sense as they were intended.

3. IT IS PARTICULARLY IMPORTANT that we take great care about the word "in" and the word "up," for the misunderstanding of these two words is the source of considerable error and hypocrisy on the part of those who seek to be spiritual workers. I know this partly from my own experience and partly from what I have heard from others; and I would like to tell you something about these errors as they seem to be.

4. IT IS COMMON that when a young disciple leaves the world to enter the school of God, he believes that when he has given himself for a little while to penance and to prayer and has taken counsel in confession, he is then capable of undertaking the spiritual work of which he hears people around him speaking and reading and which he himself perhaps reads. When such young disciples read or hear people speaking of the spiritual work—and particularly when they hear such phrases as: "how a man shall draw all his senses within himself" or "how he shall climb above himself," they misunderstand these words altogether because of the blindness of their souls and the sensual curiosity of their minds; and then, because they have in themselves a natural desire to know hidden things, they believe that they have been called to the work they grace.

5. IN FACT, if the advice of their teachers does not agree with their wish to undertake the work, they begin to complain about their teachers and they think—and perhaps they even say so to others—that they cannot find anyone who really understands them. As a result of this bold and presumptuous curiosity of their minds, they discontinue their humble prayers and penance much too soon, and they undertake—at least so they think—a full spiritual work within their souls. This work, however, if it is correctly understood, is neither a physical nor a spiritual work. It is rather, to put it briefly, a working against nature, and the devil is the leading party in this work. It is the most direct road to death both of the body and of the soul; for it is foolishness and not wisdom, and it can even lead a man to madness. But they do not think that this is the case, for they undertake in this work to think of nothing but God.

CHAPTER LII

How young, presumptuous disciples
misunderstand the word "in," and the
errors that result

1. THIS IS THE WAY that the madness of which I speak is brought about. They read and hear it said that they should stop working outwardly with their senses but should work inwardly; and since they do not know what true inward working is, they work wrong. They turn their physical senses inward to their body against the course of nature, straining themselves in trying to look inward with their physical eyes and hear inward with their physical ears and so on with all their senses, trying to smell, taste, and feel inwardly.

2. BY DOING THIS they go counter to the course of nature and because of their curiosity they make their imagination labor with such a lack of discretion that they eventually turn their brains in their heads. And as soon as this happens, the devil is able to trick them with false lights and sounds, with sweet smells in their noses, with wonderful tastes in their mouths, and with many strange sensations

and burnings in their physical breasts or in their bowels, in their backs, in their kidneys, or in their limbs.

3. IN THIS FANTASY, however, they think that they have a sustaining remembrance of their God without being hindered by any vain thoughts; and this may certainly be so, for they are so filled with falsehood that vanity cannot intrude. And why? The reason is that the same devil who would give them their vain thoughts if they were working in the proper way is also the chief agent in this work. And you can be quite sure that he is not going to disturb his own work. He therefore does not take the remembrance of God away from them, for fear that he then would be suspected.

CHAPTER LIII

Concerning the various improper practices of those who do not follow this
book

1. MANY AMAZING PRACTICES are found among those
who are deceived into doing this false work in any of its
varieties, much more than are found among God's true
disciples who always follow proper practices both physically and spiritually. But it is quite different with these
others.

2. ANYONE WHO WOULD WATCH THEM while they
are sitting at their work would see, if it happened that
their eyelids were open, that they were staring as though
they were mad and they would look as though they saw
the devil. Certainly you should be careful, for the fiend
is not far off. Some of them draw their eyes up into their
heads as though they were stupid sheep beaten over the
head and about to die at any moment. Some hang their
heads on one side as though they had a worm in their ears.
Some squeak when they should speak, as though they had
no spirit in their bodies; and this is the proper condition of

a hypocrite. Some cry and whine in their throats because of their greed and haste to say what they think. And this is the condition of heretics who with presumption and sophistries of mind will always maintain error.

3. MANY UNRESTRAINED AND IMPROPER PRACTICES are the result of this error which everyone can see. Some are so careful, however, that they can stop their practices when they come before other men. But if these men could be seen in a place where they feel at ease, then I believe they would not hide their ways. I think, further, that if anyone would directly contradict their opinion they would burst forth in argument, and yet they think that all they ever do is for the love of God and to maintain the truth. Now I fully expect that unless God brings a merciful miracle so that they soon will stop, they will love God so long in this manner that they will go staring mad to the devil.

4. I DO NOT CLAIM that the devil possesses so perfect a servant as to be deceived and infected by all the fantasies that I have described here. It may well be, however, that there is one, and perhaps many, who are infected by them all. But I claim that there is no real hypocrite or heretic upon the earth who is not guilty in some degree of what I have described.

5. THERE ARE SOME MEN who are encumbered by very strange habits in their bodily bearing. When they hear something, they twist the head to one side in an odd way and tilt the chin upward, gaping with the mouth open as

though they were going to hear with the mouth instead of with the ears. There are some who, when they go to speak, tap with their fingers either on their fingers or upon their breasts, or upon the breast of the person to whom they are speaking. Others can neither sit still, stand still, nor lie still without waggling their feet or else doing something with their hands. Some move their arms in rhythm with their speaking, as though they were swimming across a great body of water. And there are some who are constantly laughing or smiling at every other word they speak as though they were giggling girls or jesting jugglers and did not know how to behave. Such joyousness would be good and proper if it were accompanied by a sober and modest bearing of the body and a happy attitude.

6. I DO NOT SAY that all these improper practices are great sins in themselves, nor that all who do these things are great sinners. But I do say that if these improper and unrestrained practices dominate the character of the man who does them, to the extent that he cannot desist from them when he wishes to, then I say that they are signs of pride, of a curious mind, and of an unregulated display and desire for knowledge. Especially, they are tokens of an instability of heart and a restlessness of mind that is especially lacking in the work of this book. The only reason for which I have discussed so many of these deceptions here in this book is in order that spiritual workers shall be able to test their work by them.

CHAPTER LIV

How, by virtue of this book, a man is
regulated by wisdom and is made excellent both in mind and body

1. ANYONE WHO TAKES PART in this work will find
that it regulates his conduct so agreeably, both in body and
in soul, that it will make him most attractive to every man
or woman who sees him. In fact, if a person who was held
in the very lowest regard should be drawn by grace to
undertake this work, his appearance would suddenly and
marvelously be changed so that all good men who saw him
would be most happy to have him in their company and
would feel that his presence was pleasing to the spirit and
would raise them in God's grace.

2. THEREFORE, whoever is able to secure this gift by
grace, let him do so; for any man who truly has it is able
to regulate himself and all that belongs to him by means
of it. He would be well able to render judgment, if the
need should arise, for people of all natures and dispositions.
He would be well able to bring himself into harmony with
all those who come into contact with him, whether they

are habitual sinners or not; and he would not fall into sin himself. Drawing the admiration of all who saw him, he would be able to lead others by the help of grace to work in the same spirit in which he works himself.

3. HIS DEMEANOR AND WORDS would be full of spiritual wisdom, full of zeal and usefulness, words spoken in sober steadfastness without any falsehood and far from the pretenses and shams of hypocrites. For there are some who devote all their capacities, both inner and outer, to thinking how they can pad their speech with many meek, suppliant words and with gestures of devotion; but. they are more concerned to seem holy in the sight of men than to be holy in the sight of God and of His angels.

4. THE REASON FOR THIS IS that these people consider it more important and take more trouble over an improper gesture or an improper word spoken out of place before men than for a thousand vain thoughts and stinking stirrings of sin drawn willfully upon themselves and expressed carelessly in the sight of God, the saints, and the angels in heaven. O Lord God, surely there must be pride on the inside when such meek words are so copious on the outside.

5. I AGREE that it is fitting and proper for those who are humble within to display suitably humble words and gestures on the outside in accordance with the humility that is within their hearts. But I do not say that these words shall be spoken in broken or in squeaking voices, in clear contrast to the natural disposition of those who speak them. If what they are saying is true, then these words should

be spoken steadfastly in a firm voice and in the wholeness of spirit of those who speak them. If a man who has by nature a clear and openly loud voice should speak these words poorly and in squeaking tones—unless, that is, he is physically ill or it is a secret between him and his God or his confessor—then it is a strong token of hypocrisy; and I include in this hypocrites both old and young.

6. WHAT MORE SHALL I SAY of these venomous deceptions? I truly believe that unless they have the grace to stop such squealing hypocrisy, their unfortunate souls, caught between the pride hidden in their hearts within and those humble words outside, will very soon sink into sorrow.

CHAPTER LV

How those who follow the fervor of
their spirits and condemn others are
deceived

1. THE DEVIL DECEIVES SOME MEN in the following
way. Most marvelously, he fires their minds with a desire
to maintain God's law and to destroy sin in all other men.
He never tempts them with a thing that is openly evil,
but he makes them like busy prelates watching over all
degrees of Christian men's living, as an abbot watches over
his monks. They censure all men for their faults, just as
though they had charge of their souls. They think they
are doing nothing for God unless they tell them all the
faults they see, and they claim that they are stirred to do
this by the fire of charity and by God's love in their hearts.
The truth is, however, that they are lying, for they are
stirred to do this by the fire of hell welling in their brains
and in their imagination.

2. THAT THIS IS SO is indicated by the following. The
devil is a spirit, and of his own nature he does not have
a body any more than an angel does. Nevertheless, when

he or an angel would take a body with God's permission in order to perform some act for any man in this life, the quality of his body corresponds, at least in part, to the kind of work he is doing.

3. THE HOLY SCRIPTURES give us an example of this. In the Old Testament and in the New Testament as well, whenever an angel was sent in a bodily form, it always disclosed either by its name or by some instrument or quality of its body what its purpose or its message was in spirit. The same is true of the devil. When he appears in a body, he represents in some quality of his body what his servants are in spirit.

4. A SINGLE EXAMPLE of this will take the place of many. In the case of some disciples of necromancy, those who have studied the calling up of wicked spirits and to some of whom the devil has appeared in bodily form, I have observed that the bodily form in which the devil appears always has one nostril that is both large and wide, and he will gladly open it up so that a man can look into it right up to the brain in his head. This brain is nothing else than the fire of hell, for the devil can have no other kind of brain than that. And if he can get a man to look into the fire of hell, that is all he wants; for with that one look, the man will lose his senses forever. But a trained disciple of necromancy knows this well enough, and he is therefore able to keep things in control and not provoke the devil.

5. THAT IS WHY I SAY and have said that whenever the

devil takes a body, he represents in some quality of his body what his servants are in spirit. He so enflames the imagination of his contemplatives with the fire of hell that suddenly without any consideration they shoot out their strange ideas; and without any reason they take it upon themselves to censure other men's faults much too soon; and they do this because they have only one nostril spiritually.

6. THE DIVISION that is in a man's nose physically separating one nostril from the other is a token of the fact that man is to have spiritual judgment and is to distinguish the good from the evil, the evil from the worse, and the good from the better before he gives any full judgment of anything that he has heard or seen done or spoken about him. And by a man's brain, imagination is what is understood spiritually; for by its nature it dwells and works in the head.

CHAPTER LVI

How men are deceived when they
incline more to their natural knowledge
and to the learning gained in the school
of men than to the common doctrine
and counsel of the Holy Church

1. THERE ARE SOME who are not deceived in the way
that has been described above, but who leave the common
doctrine and guidance of the Holy Church because of the
pride and curiosity of their minds and because of scholarly
arts. These men with all those who support them depend
much too much upon their own knowledge. Since they
were never grounded in meek blind feeling and in virtuous
living, they have been subject to a false feeling and delu-
sion created by their spiritual enemy. And, because of this,
they eventually burst up and blaspheme all the saints, the
sacraments, the statutes and ordinances of the Holy Church.
Sensual men living in the world who think that the statutes
of the Holy Church are too hard to live by turn to these
heretics quickly and easily and stalwartly maintain them,
thinking that they will be led to an easier path than is
ordained by the Holy Church.

2. Now truly I maintain that whoever will not go the hard way to heaven will go the easy way to hell. Each man must experience this for himself, for I believe that all such heretics and all their followers, if they could clearly be seen as they shall be on the last day, would be seen to be covered over with the great and horrible sins of the world in their foul flesh, secretly, in addition to their open presumption in maintaining error. They may quite properly be called the disciples of the anti-Christ, for it is said of them that despite their false fairness in public they are foul lechers in private.

CHAPTER LVII

How young, presumptuous disciples
misunderstand the word "up," and the
errors that result

1. LET US SPEAK NO MORE of these things now but continue with our subject of how young and presumptuous spiritual disciples misunderstand the word "up."

2. WHEN THEY READ OR HEAR other persons read or say that men should "lift up their hearts to God," they immediately begin to stare at the stars as though they were above the moon and they listen as though to hear angels singing in heaven. Sometimes, in the fantasy of their imaginations, these men pierce the planets and make a hole in the firmament through which to look. Then they create a God to fit their desires, clothe Him in rich garments, and set Him upon a throne far more precisely than He was ever depicted upon earth.

3. THESE MEN MAKE ANGELS in bodily forms and set about each one a varied company of musicians in much

greater detail than was ever seen or heard in this life; for the devil will deceive some of these men in amazing ways. He sends a species of dew—they believe it to be the food of angels—which comes as though out of the air falling softly and sweetly into their mouths. That is why it is their custom to sit gaping as though they were catching flies.

4. CERTAINLY ALL THIS is nothing other than deception, no matter how holy it may seem; for in time they leave all souls devoid of any true devotion. Much vanity and falsehood is in their hearts because of their false way of working. In fact, the devil often feigns strange sounds in their ears, strange lights in their eyes, and unusual smells in their noses. But all this is nothing more than falsehood.

5. THAT IS NOT, however, what they believe. They think that in this upward looking and working they are following the example of Saint Martin who saw God clad in His mantle standing among His angels, and the example of Saint Stephen who saw our Lord stand in heaven, as well as many others. And they claim the example of Christ who ascended bodily to heaven, as witnessed by His disciples. That is why they say we should turn our eyes upward.

6. I QUITE AGREE that in our physical observance we should lift up our eyes and our hands if we are stirred in spirit. But I say that the work of our spirit is to be directed neither upward nor downward, neither to one side nor to

the other, neither forward nor backward, as it would be with a physical thing. The reason is that our work should be spiritual and not physical, and it should not be carried out in a physical way.

CHAPTER LVIII

That a man should not take Saint Martin
and Saint Stephen as his example and
strain his imagination physically upward
when in prayer

1. LET US CONSIDER what is said about Saint Martin and Saint Stephen. Although they did see those things with their physical eyes, it was disclosed to them only in a miracle and in order to certify a spiritual thing.

2. THEY KNOW PERFECTLY well that Saint Martin's mantle did not actually come upon Christ's own body, for He did not need it in order to keep from being cold. Rather it came as a miracle symbolically for all of us who are capable of being saved and of being spiritually united with the body of Christ. Whoever clothes a poor man or does any other good deed for the love of God, either physically or spiritually, for any one who is in need, may be sure that he is doing that deed to Christ spiritually; and he shall be rewarded for it as substantially as though he had done it to Christ's own body. He says that Himself in the gospel.

3. HE DID NOT CONSIDER that to be enough in itself, however, and so He affirmed it afterward by a miracle. That is why He showed Himself to Saint Martin by a revelation. All the revelations that any man has ever seen in a physical form here in this life have had a spiritual meaning. And I believe that if those to whom they were disclosed had been spiritual enough, or if they had been able to perceive their significance spiritually, the revelations would never have been displayed in physical form. Let us therefore pick off the rough bark and feed ourselves upon the sweet kernel within.

4. HOW IS THIS TO BE DONE? Not as the heretics do, for they may be compared to madmen who throw their cups to the wall and break them as soon as they have had their drink. We should not do this. We should not eat the fruit in such a way that we come to despise the tree. Nor should we drink in such a way that we break the cup when we have drunk. I call the tree and the cup the visible miracle, and all proper physical observances that accord with the work of the spirit and do not hinder it. The fruit and the drink I call the spiritual meaning of these visible miracles, and of such proper physical observances as lifting up our eyes and our hands to heaven. If they are done by a spontaneous stirring of the spirit, they are good; otherwise they are hypocrisy and they are false. If they are true and contain spiritual fruit in them, why should they be despised? Men will kiss the cup that has wine in it.

5. WHAT SHALL WE SAY of this, that when our Lord ascended physically to heaven He made His way upward

into the clouds and was seen by His mother and His disciples with their physical eyes? Should we, on account of this, stare upward with our physical eyes when we do our spiritual work, looking to see Him sitting bodily in heaven or standing as Saint Stephen saw Him? Not at all. Certainly when He showed Himself to Saint Stephen physically in heaven it was not in order to instruct us to look upward toward heaven physically when doing our spiritual work to see Him there as Saint Stephen did, either standing or sitting or lying down.

6. No MAN KNOWS in what posture His body is in heaven, whether it is standing or sitting or lying down. And it is not at all necessary to know this; for all that we need to know is that His body is united with His soul and not separated. The body and the soul, which is the essence of human-ness, is also united with the Godhead and is not separated.

7. WE DO NOT NEED TO KNOW whether He is sitting, standing, or lying down, but only that He is there as He desires to be and that He is there in His body as is proper. And if He would show Himself by a revelation to any person in this life to be lying down or standing or sitting, it would be done only to convey some spiritual message and not because of the kind of physical posture He has in heaven.

8. WE CAN SEE THIS by an example. By standing is to be understood a readiness. Thus it is often said by one friend to another when they are in physical battle, "Stand up

well, fellow, fight hard and do not give up easily. I shall stand by you." By this he means not only physical standing, for it may be that the battle is on horseback or on foot, and it may be that the battle is in movement and not standing still. What he means when he says that he will stand by him is that he will be ready to help him. This was the reason for which our Lord showed Himself physically in heaven to Saint Stephen when he was enduring his martyrdom, and it was not to teach us to look up to heaven.

9. HE HAD SPOKEN in this way to Saint Stephen as a representative of all those who suffer persecution for His love. "Lo, Stephen! as truly as I open this physical firmament which is called heaven and let you see My physical standing, trust steadfastly that I am truly standing beside you spiritually with the might of My Godhead. I am ready to help you. Therefore be staunch in your faith, and endure with strength the cruel buffetings of those hard stones. Your reward will be that I shall crown you in bliss, and not only you, but all those who suffer persecution in any form for Me." From this you can see that those physical revelations were made with spiritual meanings.

CHAPTER LIX

That a man should not take the bodily
ascension of Christ as his example, to
strain his imagination upwards physically when in prayer; and that time,
place, and body should all be forgotten
in this spiritual work.

1. IF YOU SPEAK of the ascension of our Lord saying
that it was performed physically with both a physical and
a spiritual meaning since He ascended both as God and as
man, this is what I will answer you. He had been dead and
He was clothed with immortality, just as we shall be on
judgment day.

2. AT THAT TIME we shall be made so fine both in body
and in soul that we shall be able to go physically wherever
we wish as swiftly as we are able to go there now spiritually in our thoughts, whether it be up or down, to one
side or the other, behind or before. All, as the scholars say,
will then, I think, be equally good. Now, however, you
cannot come to heaven physically, but only spiritually.
And this must be so spiritual that it cannot be in any

physical manner at all, neither upward nor downward, neither to one side nor to the other, neither forward nor behind.

3. ALL THOSE WHO UNDERTAKE to be spiritual workers and particularly those who follow the work of this book must understand fully that although they read *"lift up"* or *"go in,"* and even though the work of this book is called a *"stirring,"* they must be constantly aware that this stirring reaches neither *up* nor *in* in a physical way, and that it is not the kind of stirring that moves from one place to another. Even though it is sometimes referred to as a *rest,* you must not think that it is the kind of rest in which you remain in one place without moving. In its perfection this work is so pure and so spiritual in itself that, when you conceive it correctly, you can easily see that it involves something altogether different from a physical stirring or from a physical place.

4. IT WOULD BE MUCH BETTER to refer to it as a sudden *changing* than as a stirring, or moving, of place. Time, place, and body: these three should be forgotten in all spiritual work. Be very careful in this work, therefore, and be sure not to take as your example the physical ascension of Christ so that you strain your imagination when you pray, trying to move upward physically as though you were trying to climb over the moon.

5. FROM THE SPIRITUAL POINT OF VIEW, it should not be done that way at all. Only if you could actually ascend physically to heaven, as Christ did, would it be correct for

you to follow that example. No man can do that, however, but only God, as He Himself testifies, saying, "There is no man who may ascend to heaven, but only He who descended from heaven and became man for the love of man." If this were possible for man at all, as it is not in any case, it would be so only because of very great spiritual work done in the power of the spirit; and it would be very far indeed from any stressing and straining of the imagination physically either up, or in, or to one side or the other. Therefore leave such falsehood alone. It is not so.

CHAPTER LX

That the high way and the closest way
to heaven is run by desires and not by
paces of feet

1. NOW PERHAPS YOU SAY, how then should it be? It seems to you that you have ample evidence that heaven is upward. Certainly Christ ascended into the air upward physically, and He sent the Holy Ghost as He had promised, coming from above physically, and all His disciples saw it. This is our belief. You think, therefore, that since you have this evidence, why should you not direct your mind upward physically when you pray.

2. TO THIS I WILL ANSWER as humbly as I can as follows. Since it was so that Christ did ascend physically and then sent the Holy Ghost physically, it was only proper that it be upward and from above rather than downward and from underneath, or behind, or before, or on one side or the other. Apart from this, however, He had no more need to go upward than to have gone downward. I mean, with respect to the nearness of the way.

3. FROM THE SPIRITUAL POINT OF VIEW, heaven is as much down as up, and as much up as down; as much behind as before, and as much before as behind; and as much to one side as to any other. In fact, whoever has a true desire to be in heaven is in heaven spiritually at that very time. The high road there which is the shortest road there is run in terms of desires and not of paces of feet.

4. THAT IS WHY Saint Paul has said of himself and of many others that even though our bodies are here on earth at the present time, nonetheless our life is in heaven. He was referring to their love and their desire, which is their life spiritually. Certainly a soul is as truly there when its love is as it is in the body that lives by means of it and to which it gives life. Therefore, if we wish to go to heaven spiritually, it is not necessary to strain our spirit either up or down, not to one side nor to the other.

CHAPTER LXI

That all physical things are subject to
spiritual things and are ruled according to the course of nature, and not
contrariwise

1. IT IS NECESSARY, however, that we do lift our
eyes and our hands physically upward as though toward
that physical heaven in which the elements are contained.
But we are to do so only if we are impelled to it by the
work in our spirit, and otherwise not. Physical things
depend on spiritual things and must be regulated on that
principle, not on its opposite.

2. AN EXAMPLE OF THIS can be seen in the ascension
of our Lord. When the appointed time had come for Him
to return to His Father physically with His manhood,
which never was and never can be absent from His
divinity, then, by virtue of the great power of the divine
spirit, the manhood in the body went along in the unity of
the person. And this, quite properly, was seen to be
upward.

3. THE SAME SUBJECTION of the body to the spirit may also be perceived in a true form by those who are engaged in practicing the spiritual work of this book. Whenever a soul gives himself effectively to this work, he finds at once, suddenly and without his knowing what brought it about, that his body, which had been bent downward somewhat before he had begun the work, is now set upright by virtue of the spirit, following in physical correspondence the style of the spiritual work. And it is quite proper that it should be so.

4. THIS IS MOST BECOMING TO MAN, and it is because of this that man, who is the best-looking creature that God ever made, is not made bending toward the earth as all other animals are, but is made upright in the direction of heaven. And why is this so? In order to represent in physical form the spiritual work of the soul, a work that is possible only for those who are upright spiritually and are not spiritually bent toward the ground. Take note that I say upright spiritually and not physically, for how can a soul whose nature has nothing physical in it be drawn upright in a physical way? No, that never can be so.

5. BE VERY CAREFUL, therefore, not to understand in a physical way what is meant spiritually, even though it is spoken in physical words such as up or down, in or out, behind or before, on one side or the other. No matter how spiritual a thing may be in itself, it is unavoidable that if it is to be spoken of at all it must necessarily be spoken of with physical words, since speech is a work of the body performed by the tongue, which is an instrument of the

body. But what of that? Does that mean that it should, therefore, be interpreted in a physical way? Not at all; it should be interpreted spiritually, as it was intended to be.

CHAPTER LXII

How a man may know when his
spiritual work is beneath him or outside
of him, when it is even with him or
within him, and when it is above him
and under his God

1. To this end, in order that you will be better able to
know how these words that are spoken physically are to
be understood spiritually, I will now explain to you the
spiritual significance of some words that occur in spiritual
work. Then you will be able to know clearly and without
error when your spiritual work is beneath you and outside
you, when it is within you and even with you, and when
it is above you and under your God.

2. Everything physical is outside your soul and
beneath it in nature. This is true even of the sun and the
moon and all the stars. Although they are above your
body, they are nevertheless beneath your soul.

3. All angels and all souls whose grace has been con-
firmed and who are bedecked with many virtues are above
you in purity. But they are only equal to you in nature.

4. WITHIN YOURSELF IN NATURE there are the powers of your soul. The three principal ones are: Memory, Reason, and Will. The secondary ones are Imagination and Sensuality.

5. NOTHING AT ALL is above you in nature, but only God.

6. WHENEVER YOU FIND the word "yourself" used in spiritual writing, understand it to mean your soul and not your body. The value and quality of your work is then to be judged by this, according to the level on which the powers of your soul are functioning. This will tell whether your work is beneath you, within you, or above you.

CHAPTER LXIII

Concerning the powers of the soul in
general, and how memory in particular
is a principal power comprehending
within it all the other powers and all
those things in which they work

1. MEMORY IS A TYPE OF POWER which, properly speaking, cannot be said to work of itself. Reason and Will, however, are two working powers, and Imagination and Sensuality are two more. All these four powers and their works are contained in memory and are comprehended in it. Other than this we cannot say that the memory works, unless this quality of containing can be called a work.*

2. BECAUSE OF THIS I call some of the powers of the soul principal and some secondary. This is not because a soul is divisible, for that is not so at all. It is because the areas

---

* [The reader should keep in mind that the term "memory" is used here in a sense that is much more extensive than its modern usage. It refers to the dynamic quality of the conscious mind as a whole. The direct source of this conception is St. Augustine, and a close equivalent to it in modern philosophy would be the *memoire* of Henri Bergson. I.P.]

in which the soul works may be divided one from the other, some being principal as are all spiritual things, and some being secondary, as are all physical things.

3. THE TWO PRINCIPAL WORKING POWERS, Reason and Will, work altogether of themselves in all spiritual things without the help of the two secondary powers. Imagination and Sensuality work on an animal level in all physical things, whether they be present or absent. They work in the body using the body's senses. By them alone, however, without the help of Reason and Will, a person can never come to know the nature and condition of physical creatures, nor the source of their existence and their creation.

4. BECAUSE OF THIS, Reason and Will are called the principal powers, for they work altogether in the spirit without anything of a physical nature. Imagination and Sensuality are classed as secondary because they work in the body, using the bodily instruments that are called our five senses. Memory is called a principal power because there is contained within it spiritually not only all the other powers but all the things with which they do their work. You can verify this by your own experience.

CHAPTER LXIV

Concerning the two other principal
powers, Reason and Will, and of their
work before sin and after sin

1. REASON IS THE POWER by means of which we separate evil from good, the evil from the worse, the good from the better, the worse from the worst, and the better from the best. Before man had sinned, Reason may have been able to do all this by its own nature. Now, however, it is so blinded as a result of the original sin that it is not capable of doing this work unless it is illumined by grace. And now, both Reason itself and the things with which it works are comprehended by and are contained in the memory.

2. WILL IS A POWER by means of which we choose the good after that has been determined by Reason. By means of it, also, we love the good, we desire the good, and we rest ourselves with full pleasure and consent ultimately in God. Before man had sinned, the Will could not be deceived in its choosing, in its loving, nor in any of its works, for it was then able by its very nature to know each thing

as it was. It cannot now do that, however, unless it has been anointed with grace. Very often now because of the infection of the original sin, it judges a thing to be good when it is exceedingly evil and has only the appearance of good. And both the will and the thing that is willed are contained and comprehended in the Memory.

CHAPTER LXV

Concerning the first secondary power,
Imagination, its works and its obedience
to Reason, before sin and after sin

1. IMAGINATION IS A POWER by means of which we portray the images of all absent and present things; and both it and the things that it portrays are contained in the Memory. Before man had sinned, the Imagination was obedient to the Reason to which it was like a servant, never bringing to it any unauthorized image of a physical creature; but now that is no longer the case.

2. Now, UNLESS IT IS RESTRAINED by the light of grace in the reason, the Imagination will never cease, whether in sleep or in waking, to portray various unauthorized images of physical creatures, or else some fantasy that is nothing else than a physical conception of a spiritual thing. And this lends itself increasingly to invention and falsity, leading soon to error.

3. THIS DISOBEDIENCE OF THE IMAGINATION can be clearly seen in the prayers of those who have newly turned

from the world to the life of devotion. Before the Imagination has been restrained to a significant degree by the light of grace in the Reason as is achieved by constant meditation on spiritual subjects—such as their own wretchedness, the passion and the kindness of our Lord God, and many similar things—they are completely unable to put away the amazing and varied thoughts, fantasies, and images that are brought to their minds and impressed upon them by the light of curiosity of Imagination. And all this disobedience is the result of the original sin.

CHAPTER LXVI

Concerning the other secondary power,
Sensuality, its works and its obedience
to the Will, before sin and after sin

1. SENSUALITY IS THE POWER of our soul that guides
and controls our physical senses and by means of which
we have bodily knowledge of all physical creatures, those
who please us and those who do not. It has two parts. By
one, it gives attention to the needs of the body; by the
other, it serves the lusts of the physical senses.

2. IT IS THIS POWER that complains when the body lacks
any of the things that are necessary for it; and also, in
taking account of the need, it stirs us to take more than
is necessary in feeding and furthering our lusts. It complains at the absence of pleasant creatures, and it is highly
delighted when they are present. It complains of the presence of creatures it dislikes, and it is greatly pleased by
their absence. Both this power and the things in which it
works are contained in the Memory.

3. BEFORE MAN HAD COMMITTED the original sin, Sen-

suality was so obedient to the Will to which it was as a servant that it never brought it to any improper pleasure or complaint with respect to any physical creature, nor to any spiritual expression of liking or disliking as might be wrought by the devil in the physical senses. But now that is no longer the case.

4. Now, UNLESS SENSUALITY IS GOVERNED by grace in the Will, so that it will endure with meekness and with moderation the consequences of the original sin that are visited upon it as the absence of necessary comforts and as the presence of unavoidable discomforts, it will not be restrained from lustful pleasures in these things. Then it will welter wretchedly and wantonly as a swine in the mire in the wealth of this world and in the foul flesh to such an extent that our life will be more animal and carnal than either human or spiritual.

CHAPTER LXVII

That whoever does not know the powers of a soul and her manner of working may easily be deceived in understanding spiritual words and spiritual works; and how a soul is made a God in grace

1. Lo, SPIRITUAL FRIEND, to such wretchedness as you may see here have we fallen because of sin. It is small wonder, therefore, that we are blindly and easily deceived in our understanding of spiritual words and spiritual working. And this is particularly the case with those who are not aware of the powers of their soul and the modes of their operation.

2. WHENEVER THE MEMORY is occupied with any physical thing, no matter how good the purpose may be, you are beneath yourself in that act and you are outside your soul.

3. WHENEVER YOU FEEL your memory to be occupied with the subtle qualities of the powers of your soul and

their way of operation in spiritual things, such as vices or virtues whether of yourself or of any other creature who is spiritually your equal; and whenever your aim in this is to learn to know yourself in order to work better toward perfection, you are then within yourself and even with yourself.

4. But whenever you feel your Memory to be occupied with nothing physical and with nothing spiritual but only with the very substance of God, as it is and may be in the practice of the work of this book, then you are above yourself and you are beneath your God.

5. You are above yourself. And why do I say that? Because you have then attained by grace a state that you cannot reach by nature. That is to say, to be united with God in spirit, and in love, and in harmony of will.

6. You are beneath your God. And why is that? It is true that in a sense you and God at this time are not two but are one in spirit. In fact, you or any other person who by such an act of unification has reached the perfection of this work may certainly on the testimony of Scripture be called a God. But you are beneath God all the same. The reason is that He is God by nature without beginning. You, on the other hand, were nothing at all at one time and after you had been made into something by His might and His love, you willfully with sin made yourself worse than nothing. And now only by His mercy and not because of your merit you are made a God in grace, united with Him in spirit without separation, both here and in the

bliss of heaven without any end. Thus it is that although you are completely one with Him in grace, you are nevertheless very far beneath Him in nature.

7. Lo, SPIRITUAL FRIEND, by this you can see at least partially that whoever does not know the powers of his own soul and the manner of their operation can very easily be deceived in understanding words that are written with a spiritual meaning. You can thus see a part of the reason for which I dared not tell you to display your desire for God plainly, but instead I bade you childishly to do whatever you can to hide it and cover it as in the manner of a child. And I do this for fear that you will understand in a physical way what is meant spiritually.

CHAPTER LXVIII

That nowhere physically is everywhere
spiritually, and how the outer man calls
the work of this book nothing

1. IN THE SAME SENSE, where another man would tell
you to gather your powers and your senses altogether
within yourself and worship God there, I would not tell
you to do that. He would be speaking truly in saying that;
in fact, if he were correctly understood, no man could
speak more truly. But I would be afraid that you would
come into error by interpreting his words physically. This,
rather, is what I will tell you. Take care that not in any
manner will you be within yourself. And also I do not
want you to be outside of yourself, and not above yourself, nor behind yourself, and not on one side nor on the
other.

2. "WHERE THEN," you say, "shall I be? Nowhere,
according to you!" Now truly you speak well; for that
is exactly where I would have you be. The reason is that
nowhere physically is everywhere spiritually. Take great

care then that your spiritual work is nowhere physically, and then no matter where the thing on which you are consciously working may be, you will surely be there in spirit as truly as your body is in the place where you are physically.

3. EVEN THOUGH YOUR PHYSICAL SENSES can find nothing there on which to feed themselves for they think that you are doing nothing, continue doing this nothing, and do it for the love of God. Do not give up, but labor on with great effort in that nothing with a strong desire and a will to have God whom no man can know. I tell you truly that I would rather be nowhere physically in this way, wrestling with that blind nothing, than to be so great a lord that I could be wherever I wished physically, merrily playing with all this something as a lord with his own.

4. LEAVE THIS EVERYWHERE and this something alone and choose this nowhere and this nothing. Do not be concerned if your mind cannot reason about this nothing; for certainly I love it much the better. It is so valuable a thing in itself that no one can reason about it. This nothing can be felt more easily than it can be seen, for it brings a blinding darkness to those who look at it for even a little while. Nevertheless, to tell the truth, a person is more blinded in his feeling for it when he has great spiritual light than when he is in darkness and lacks physical light.

5. AND WHO IS IT that calls this nothing? Surely it is our

outer man and not our inner man. Our inner man calls it All, for it teaches him to know the essence of all things, both physical and spiritual, with no special attention to any one thing by itself.

CHAPTER LXIX

How a man's affection is marvelously
changed in the spiritual feeling of this
nothing, when it is done nowhere

1. A MAN IS WONDERFULLY CHANGED by the spiritual
experience of this nothing when it is accomplished nowhere. At the first moment that a person looks upon it,
he sees secretly or darkly painted upon it all the special
acts of sin, physical and spiritual, that he has committed
since he was born. No matter how he turned it around,
they will still appear before his eyes until finally, after
much hard labor, intense grieving, and many bitter tears,
he has finally washed most of them away.

2. SOMETIMES IN THE COURSE of this labor it seems to
him that it is as though he were looking upon hell, for he
thinks that he has no hope of ever achieving his goal of
spiritual perfection and peace out of that pain. There are
many who come this far inward, but because the pain they
feel is so great and because they miss their pleasures, they
let their attention return to physical things. Then they
seek sensual pleasures on the outside once again in place

of the spiritual ones they have not yet achieved but which they would have achieved had they continued.

3. THE MAN WHO CONTINUES in the work eventually feels some pleasure and has some expectation of perfection, for he sees that many of the special sins he had committed in the past are rubbed away by the help of grace. He continues to feel pain, but he thinks that it will come to an end since it is becoming less and less. He considers it, therefore, to be nothing else than purgatory.

4. SOMETIMES HE CAN FIND no special sin shown to him, and yet he knows that sin is a *lump*, he knows not what, and that it is nothing else than himself. This is the base and pain of the original sin. Sometimes it seems to him that it is paradise or heaven because of the many wonderful sweetnesses and pleasures, joys and blessed virtues, that he finds in it. Sometimes it seems to him to be God because of the peace and rest that he finds in it.

5. YES, LET HIM THINK whatever he wishes. He will always find that it is *a cloud of unknowing* between him and his God.

CHAPTER LXX

That just as by failing in our spiritual
senses we begin to come to a better
knowledge of spiritual things, so also
by failing in our spiritual senses we
begin to come to the knowledge of
God, to the extent that it is possible·by
grace in this life

1. LABOR HARD, therefore, in this nothing and in this
nowhere and turn away from your outward physical
senses and all things with which they deal. I tell you truly
that this work cannot be comprehended by means of them.

2. YOU CANNOT CONCEIVE of anything by means of
your eyes unless it is in terms of length and breadth, small-
ness and largeness, roundness and squareness, distance and
closeness, or its color. By means of your ears you can conceive nothing except noise or some kind of sound; and
nothing by your nose but a smell, either a stench or a
savor; and nothing by your taste but sweet or sour, salt
or fresh, bitter or pleasant; and nothing by your feeling
but hot or cold, hard or soft, blunt or sharp. And it is

true that neither God nor any of these spiritual things have any of these qualities or quantities.

3. TURN AWAY THEREFORE from your outward senses and do not work with them, neither within nor outside yourself. All those who undertake to be spiritual workers within themselves and believe that they should hear, smell, or see, taste, or feel spiritual things either within or outside themselves surely are deceived and are working wrongly against the course of nature.

4. INHERENTLY IT IS SO that those who follow them achieve a knowledge of outward physical things; but they cannot possibly receive through them a knowledge of spiritual things. At least not from their accomplishments; but possibly from their failures they may. For example, when we read or hear of certain things and realize that our outward senses cannot tell us what the qualities of these things may be, we can be quite sure then that those things are spiritual things and are not physical things.

5. IT IS QUITE THE SAME in a spiritual way when we work with our spiritual senses seeking a knowledge of God Himself. No matter how much spiritual understanding a man may have in the knowledge of all created spiritual things, he can never come by means of this understanding to the knowledge of an uncreated spiritual thing. And this is nothing but God. But he may do so through his incapacity, for the thing that he is unable to know is nothing else than God.

6. IT WAS FOR THIS REASON that Saint Denis said, "The best knowledge of God is what is known by unknowing." Truly, whoever will read Denis' books will find that his words clearly affirm all that I have said or shall say from the beginning of this treatise to the end. I do not wish to cite him or any other authority, however, on any other point than this, at least at this time. Once men considered it a sign of humility to speak nothing that came from their own heads unless they could affirm it by Scripture and by the words of authorities. Now, however, that has turned into artfulness and the display of knowledge. You have no need of that, and therefore I do not do it. Whoever has ears, let him hear; and whoever is stirred to believe, let him believe. And otherwise, not.

CHAPTER LXXI

That some may feel the perfection of
this work only in a time of ecstacy,
while others may feel it whenever they
wish, in the common state of man's soul

1. SOME CONSIDER THIS UNDERTAKING to be so difficult and so awesome that it cannot be achieved without
much heavy labor. They claim, also, that it can be comprehended but very rarely, and then only in moments of
ecstasy. To these men I answer as humbly as I can and
say that it all depends on the decree and the disposition
of God. This grace of contemplation and spiritual work
is given according to the capacity of the soul.

2. THERE ARE SOME who cannot achieve it without great
and lengthy spiritual exercise; and even then it is very rare
and only by a special calling from our Lord that they can
experience the perfection of this work; and this calling is
referred to as rapture. There are, however, also some who
are so discerning in grace and in spirit and are so familiar
with God in this grace of contemplation that they may

have it whenever they wish in the ordinary state of man's soul, whether sitting, moving about, standing, or kneeling. In this command they even have full command of their senses both physical and spiritual and can use them if they so desire, not without some difficulty, but without great difficulty.

3. WE HAVE AN EXAMPLE of the first type in Moses, and of the second type in Aaron, the priest of the temple. The reason is that this grace of contemplation is symbolized by the ark of the covenant in the Old Testament, and those who worked in this grace are represented by those who mingled most around the ark, as the story indicates. It is quite appropriate to compare this grace and this work to that ark, for just as all the jewels and relics of the Temple were contained in that ark so also are all the virtues of man's soul, which is the spiritual temple of God, contained in this little love placed upon this *cloud of unknowing*.

4. BEFORE MOSES COULD SEE this ark and before he could know how it was to be made, he had to climb with long and difficult labor up to the top of the mountain. He had to remain there, struggling in the cloud for six days and waiting until the seventh day in order that the Lord would be willing to show him the way to make the ark. The long labor of Moses and the late disclosure that came to him represent those who are not able to arrive at the perfection of this spiritual work without long labor coming before, even then succeeding very seldom and only when God is willing to reveal it.

5. ALTHOUGH MOSES COULD COME to see it very seldom and then only with a great and long labor, Aaron had it in his power because of his office to see it in the Temple within the Veil whenever he wished to enter. And Aaron here represents all those of whom I have spoken above who may achieve perfection in this work whenever they desire, by means of their spiritual knowledge and with the help of grace.

CHAPTER LXXII

That a man engaged in this work should
not consider another worker to have
the same experiences as he himself has

1. FROM THIS YOU CAN REALIZE that those who are
able to see or experience the perfection of this work only
after a long labor and then but seldom may easily be
deceived if they speak, think, or judge other men in terms
of their own experience, thinking that other men are like
them able to achieve it only rarely, and then not without
great labor.

2. CORRESPONDINGLY, the man who can have it whenever he wishes will also be deceived if he judges all other
people by himself, saying that they can have it whenever
they wish. That would be very good, but he surely should
not think it is so.

3. AT SOME TIME it might very well be God's desire that
those who were at first able to have it only very seldom
and then only with great labor should afterward have it
whenever they wish and as often as they please. We have

an example of this in Moses who at first upon the mount was not able to see the nature of the ark and then only seldom and with great labor; but after that he was able to see it as often as he wished from within the veil.

CHAPTER LXXIII

In a way similar to Moses, Bezaleel, and
Aaron mingling around the ark of the
Testament, we benefit in a threefold
manner in this grace of contemplation,
for this grace is expressed in that ark

1. The three principal men who were concerned
with the ark of the Old Testament were Moses, Bezaleel,
and Aaron. Moses learned upon the mount of our Lord
how it was to be made. Bezaleel constructed it and made
it in the Veil according to the instructions that were given
on the mountain. And Aaron was in charge of it in the
Temple to feel it and see it as often as he liked.

2. In accordance with these three, we can advance in three different ways in this grace of contemplation. Sometimes we can advance only by grace, and then
we may be compared to Moses who could come to see it
only very seldom despite all the climbing and struggle he
endured to reach the mount. And even then, when it was
finally shown to him, it was only because the Lord wished

to show it to him, and not because of the merits of his labor.

3. SOMETIMES WE ADVANCE in this grace by our own spiritual adeptness helped by grace, and then we may be compared to Bezaleel who could not see the ark until the time when he had made it by his own labor, aided by the instructions that had been given to Moses on the mount.

4. AND SOMETIMES WE ADVANCE in this grace from the teachings of other men. Then we may be compared to Aaron who had it in his charge, and was able to see and feel whenever he pleased the ark that Bezaleel had constructed and had given ready-made to his hands.

5. LO, SPIRITUAL FRIEND in this work, I have described it foolishly and without learning and I know that I am a wretched man not worthy to teach any one the function of Bezaleel. That function is to make the spiritual ark, and to describe its nature and the making of it in terms of the use of your hands. But your work can be much better and of much greater value than mine if you will be as Aaron; that is, if you will continually work in this for yourself and for me. Do this, I pray of you, for the love of God Almighty. And since we have both been called by God to carry on this work, I implore you for the love of God to fulfill in your part of the work what is lacking in mine.

CHAPTER LXXIV

How it is that the subject of this book
is never heard or spoken, nor heard to
be read or to be spoken, by a person
well disposed toward it without feeling
a true sympathy with the effects of the
work; and also repeating the charge
that is written in the prologue

1. IF YOU THINK that this manner of working does not
accord well with your disposition in body and soul, you
may leave it without blame and safely take some other way
following good spiritual advice. In that case, I beg you to
excuse me, for I truly wished to be of help to you by
writing with my limited knowledge. That was my intention. Read it over, therefore, twice or three times, the
more often the better, for you will then understand it more
fully. It may be, in fact, that if there was a sentence that
was very difficult for you at the first or second reading,
you will soon afterwards find it easy.

2. INDEED, IT SEEMS IMPOSSIBLE to my understanding

that any person who is disposed to this work should read it or speak it or else hear it read or spoken without feeling a close harmony with the consequences of this work. And then if you think that it does you good, thank God with all your heart, and for the love of God pray for me.

3. Do THIS THEN. And I beg of you that for God's love you will let no one see this book except for such a person as you think is fit for this book according to what you have found written in the book earlier where it tells which men should do this work and when they should undertake it. And if you let any such men see it, then I beg of you that you tell them to take their time in reading it all over.

4. It MAY BE that there will be some subject in the beginning, or in the middle, that is left dangling and is not fully explained there as it stands. But if it is not explained there, it will be soon afterward, or else before the end. If a man sees only one part and not another, he might easily be led into error; and that is why I ask you to work as I have said. And if you think that there is any subject in this book that you would like to have discussed more fully, let me know which it is and your opinions about it; and with my simple knowledge it will be improved if I am able.

5. As FOR WORLDLY BABBLERS, however, flatterers and complainers, gossips and tale-bearers and misanthropes of every kind—I hope that they never see this book. I never had the intention of writing such a thing for them. I would

prefer, therefore, that they did not hear of it, neither they nor any of those who are merely curious whether they are learned men or not. They are very good men engaged in the active life, but this book is not for them.

CHAPTER LXXV

Concerning certain signs by which a
man may verify whether he has been
called by God to engage in this work

1. IF YOU READ THIS BOOK or hear it read or spoken of
and if you then feel that it is a good and worthwhile thing,
you should not think that you are therefore called by God
to do this work merely because you feel this stirring when
you read this book. It may be that this stirring comes from
a natural curiosity of mind rather than from the calling
of grace.

2. THOSE WHO WISH TO VERIFY the source of this stirring, however, may do so if they wish. First let them
consider whether they have worked within themselves
previously, and whether they have done anything to en-
able them to cleanse their consciousness for the judgment
of the Holy Church, in accordance with counsel.

3. IF THEY THEN WISH to know more specifically, let
them consider whether this stirring has constantly been
pressing on their minds more persistently than any other

kind of spiritual activity. And if they think that nothing else that they do, whether physical or spiritual, satisfies their consciences as being sufficient unless this secret little love pressing upon *the cloud of unknowing* is present in a spiritual way as the culmination of all their work; then, if they feel this, it is a token that they are called by God to do this work; and otherwise, not at all.

4. I DO NOT SAY that it shall last permanently and remain continually in the minds of all of those who are called to practice this work. That is not the way it is. In fact, there are several reasons for which the actual feeling of the work may often be withdrawn from young spiritual disciples. Sometimes it is withdrawn so that he shall not treat it presumptuously and believe that it is largely in his own power to have it when he desires and as he desires. Such a belief is pride, and whenever the feeling of grace is withdrawn, pride is the cause. That is to say, it is not because of pride he has actually had in the past, but because of the pride he would have if this feeling of grace were not withdrawn. Thus it is often the case that young fools think that God is their enemy, when He is completely their friend.

5. SOMETIMES IT IS WITHDRAWN because of their carelessness, and when this is the case they feel a most bitter pain soon afterward. Sometimes our Lord will delay it deliberately. By such a delay he wishes to make it grow and be valued more when it has been newly found and experienced again after it has long been lost. And this is one of the surest and most fundamental signs by which a

person can know whether or not he has been called to practice this work; that is, if he feels after such a delay and a long absence of the work that when it comes suddenly as it does, unsought by any special means, that he has then a greater strength and fervor and feels a greater love in longing to practice this work than he ever had before. When this is the case, I believe that he often has more joy in finding it than he had sorrow when he lost it.

6. AND IF THIS IS HOW IT IS, it is surely a true token with no mistake that he is called by God to practice this work, whatever he is or has been.

7. IT IS NOT WHAT YOU ARE, and not what you have been, but what you wish to be that God considers with His merciful eyes. Saint Gregory testifies that all holy desires grow by delays, and if they are diminished by delays, they were never holy desires. If a man feels less and less joy in new discoveries and in the unexpected fulfillment of old desires he had had in the past, then, even though they may have been natural desires seeking the good, they were never holy desires. Saint Austin spoke of such a holy desire when he said that the entire life of a good Christian man is nothing else but holy desire.

8. FAREWELL, SPIRITUAL FRIEND, with God's blessing and mine. I beseech Almighty God that true peace, holy counsel, and spiritual comfort in God with an abundance of grace will forever be with you and with all those upon earth who love God. Amen.

ABOUT THE AUTHOR

Both as critic of the old and as originator of new conceptions, Dr. Ira Progoff has long been in the vanguard of those who have worked toward a dynamic humanistic psychology. In his practice as therapist, in his books, as lecturer and group leader, as Bollingen Fellow, and as Director of the Institute for Research in Depth Psychology at the Graduate School of Drew University, he has conducted pioneer research and has developed major new techniques for the enlargement of human potential.

These studies have led to the founding of two significant organizations. The first is Dialogue House Associates which is devoted to using the *Intensive Journal* developed by Dr. Progoff as the basis for varied programs of personal growth in education, religion, industry, and social organization. The second is the Humanic Arts Research and Resource Center, which is devoted to developing experiential programs of advanced training for people who work in the helping and teaching professions.

The core of Ira Progoff's work is contained in a trilogy of basic books. *The Death and Rebirth of Psychology* (1956) crystallizes the cumulative results of the work of the great historical figures in depth psychology and sets the foundation for a new psychology of personal growth. *Depth Psychology and Modern Man* (1959) presents the evolutionary and philosophical perspectives, and formulates basic concepts which make creative experience possible. *The Symbolic and the Real* (1963) pursues the practical and religious implications of these ideas and applies them in techniques and disciplines which individuals may use in their personal growth.